S0-ADN-225

THE
BOOK
OF
Sea
Monsters

THE
BOOK
OF Sea
MonSters

BOB EGGLETON

Text by Nigel Suckling

The Overlook Press
Woodstock•New York

This book is dedicated to J. M. W. Turner . . .
you saw them too.
Bob Eggleton

First published in the United States in 1998
by The Overlook Press
Lewis Hollow Road
Woodstock, NY 12498

First published in Great Britain in 1998
by Paper Tiger
An imprint of Collins & Brown Limited

Copyright © Collins & Brown Limited 1998

Text copyright © Collins & Brown Limited 1998
Illustrations copyright © Bob Eggleton 1998

All Rights Reserved. No part of this publication may be reproduced or transmitted in any form,
or by any means, electronic or mechanical, including photocopy, recording or any information storage
and retrieval system now known or to be invented without permission in writing from the publisher,
except by a reviewer who wishes to quote brief passages in connection with a review written
for inclusion in a magazine, newspaper, or broadcast.

3 5 7 9 8 6 4 2

Library of Congress Cataloging-in-Publication Data

Suckling, Nigel.
The book of sea monsters / illustrated by Bob Eggleton : text by Nigel Suckling
p.   cm
ISBN 0-87951-860-X
I. Marine animals. 2. Sea monsters.   I. Eggleton, Bob.
II. Title.
QL 121.S83 1998
001.944-dc21
98-10742
CIP

Designer: Megra Mitchell, Mitchell Strange

Reproduction by Hong Kong Graphic and Printing Ltd
Printed and bound in Singapore by Kyodo Printing Co (S'pore) Pte Ltd

CONTENTS

WHY SEA MONSTERS?

Water – the sea and its mysteries – has held me in its thrall since my youth, just as I have always been fascinated by outer space and inner space. Being born under a water sign may also have something to do with this, but certainly I could never live far away from the sea. In addition, monsters hold a profound fascination for me – as if that was not obvious to anyone who has already had a preliminary browse through this book! And so *The Book of Sea Monsters* became inevitable: it was something I had to do. I asked Nigel Suckling if he would write the text and was delighted when he agreed. My challenge, of course, was to try to paint pictures as eloquent as Nigel's text. If these pictures make you look twice when you are next near an ocean or lake and see a strange ripple or splash, then maybe they have achieved their purpose.

How was I to go about things? For years I had let myself be stereotyped – I was allowing myself to become just another artist whose slick airbrush style was perfect for paperback books. My work had begun to look flat and mechanical to me; worst of all, I felt I was losing my ability to draw pictures. Like any artist worthy of the name I wanted to experiment, to assert my creativity outside the narrow confines of commercial art.

I took what with hindsight was a bold decision: I determined to change my style, to return to my artistic roots. In my search for fresh inspiration I did a great deal of research among the Old and not-so-old Masters, visiting many museums including the Boston Museum of Fine Arts, London's Tate Gallery and the Gallery of New South Wales. While some of my peers today seem to be gravitating toward the Pre-Raphaelites, the great artists who seemed to call out to me were painters of landscapes and the ocean: the likes of Thomas Moran, Albert Bierstadt and, most of all, J.M.W. Turner, to whom I have dedicated this book.

One can relatively easily become an adequate and reasonably successful illustrator – computer-imaging processes, in the wrong hands more mechanical than any airbrush, have made this even easier – and certainly there is a market for such work. By contrast, it takes a lifetime to fulfil one's potential as a true painter. As I near my midlife, this has become a more important goal than simply producing saleable pictures in order to pay the bills.

The media I used for the pictures in this book included virtually everything but the kitchen sink, and the locations where I did the work were almost as diverse. Images were produced in my studio, on the rocky cliffs of the Rhode Island coast, on beaches in south-eastern Australia, in foreign hotel rooms and, yes, on plane journeys. I used pencils, watercolours, acrylic paints and even simple black marker-pens on paper – anything to help realize my ideas. The experimentation was, as far as I'm concerned, a success. For the first time in a long while I felt like a Real Artist.

Art, for the artist, is an ongoing process, with creativity coming first and judgement later. Whether I will ever achieve the goal I share with all other serious artists, that of becoming regarded as a 'great painter', is something that obviously I can neither foresee nor judge. Nevertheless, I hope that long after I am gone, art historians will at least be charitable about the merits of my Great Moments.

Bob Eggleton

Providence, Rhode Island
February 1998

INTRODUCTION

Sea monsters have swum around the margins of the known world since time began. From the Midgard Serpent, which grew so large it circled the world entirely, to the Kraken, Leviathan and the lesser but still terrifying sea serpents logged by sober sea captains, monsters as yet unrecognized by science have been accepted through most of history as real perils of the deep.

There are literally hundreds of plausible monster sightings on record; but some stand out in particular, because of the glaring honesty of the witnesses, the strangeness of the tale or simply the impact of that tale on the public imagination. An instance that scored on all three counts was the famous Egede sighting.

The Norwegian missionary Hans Egede (1686–1758) has been dubbed 'The Apostle of Greenland' because of his role in baptizing that colony. His honesty can hardly be questioned; moreover, he was something of a marine naturalist. In his *Full and Particular Relation of My Voyage to Greenland* (1745) he describes with perfect accuracy several species of whale – including the narwhal, that shy denizen of Greenland's waters which for centuries provided Europe with 'unicorn' horns (and a lucrative sideline for the Norse sailors who kept its existence secret for so long). Egede thought he knew all the marine creatures of the north Atlantic, but one day at the latitude of 64 degrees he saw something quite new:

'Anno 1734, July. On the 6th appeared a very terrible sea-monster which raised itself so high above the water that its head reached above our main-top. It had a long, sharp snout and blew like a whale, had broad, large flappers and the body was, as it were, covered with a hard skin; and it was very wrinkled and uneven on its skin. Moreover, on

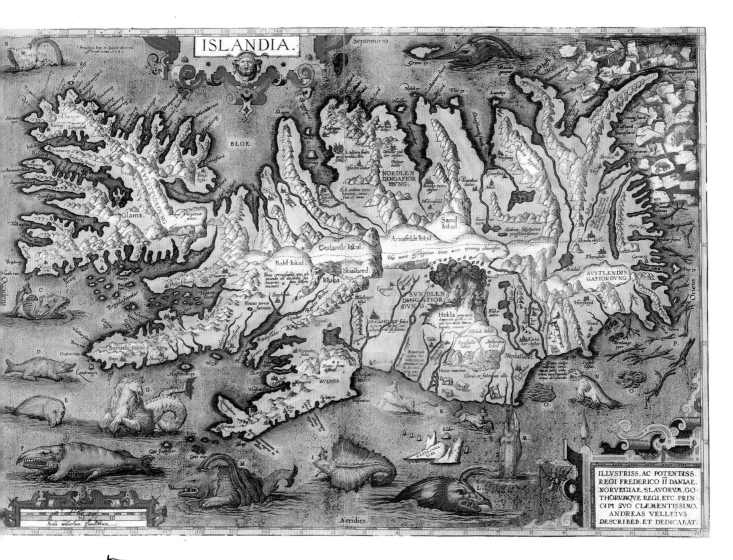

ISLANDIA.

Septemtrio

BLOE.

NORDLEN
DINGAFIOR
DVNG.

Sand
Iokul.

Arnafeldis Iokul.

AVSTLENDIN
GAFIORDVNG

Geilands Iokul.

Bald Iokul.

SVNDLEN
DINGAFIOR
DVNG.

Hekla

Medalland

Meridies

ILLVSTRISS. AC POTENTISS.
REGI FREDERICO II DANIAE.
NORVEGIAE, SLAVORVM, GO
THORVMQVE REGI, ETC. PRIN
CIPI SVO CLÆMENTISSIMO,
ANDREAS VELLEIVS
DESCRIBEB. ET DEDICABAT.

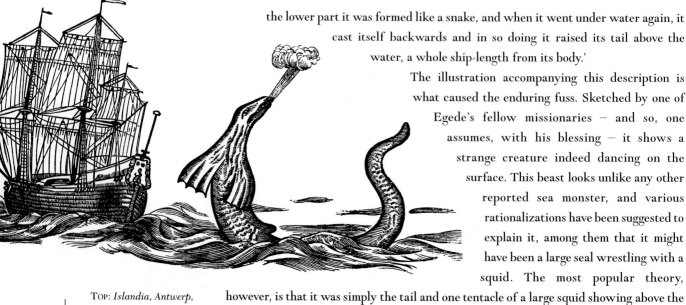

the lower part it was formed like a snake, and when it went under water again, it cast itself backwards and in so doing it raised its tail above the water, a whole ship-length from its body.'

The illustration accompanying this description is what caused the enduring fuss. Sketched by one of Egede's fellow missionaries — and so, one assumes, with his blessing — it shows a strange creature indeed dancing on the surface. This beast looks unlike any other reported sea monster, and various rationalizations have been suggested to explain it, among them that it might have been a large seal wrestling with a squid. The most popular theory, however, is that it was simply the tail and one tentacle of a large squid showing above the surface. This would mean that Egede would have to have imagined seeing the head, which must be possible, but still leaves the problem of the 'large flippers'. Moreover, a squid capable of showing 30ft (9m) of its body or mantle above water would have to be over twice the size of the largest giant squid yet found, or even suspected. So this 'rationalization' in itself ends up arguing for a monster that is beyond the pale of science.

TOP: *Islandia, Antwerp, 1595. A map charting unidentified monsters.*
ABOVE: *Hans Egede's Sea serpent (1734) seen off the coast of Greenland.*

8

An equally famous sighting is that from the British navy corvette HMS *Daedalus*. In August 1848 she was sailing about 300 miles (500km) off the coast of what is now Namibia, heading home from India, when a sea serpent passed within 100yd (90m). Rumours of the incident spread after the ship's return to England, leading to an article in *The Times* that caused the Admiralty to demand an official report from the captain. After describing the ship's exact position and the weather conditions (overcast and choppy), Captain M'Quhae had this to say:

'On our attention being called to the object, it was discovered to be an enormous serpent, with head and shoulders kept about four feet [1.2m] constantly above the surface of the sea, and as nearly as we could approximate by comparing it with the length our main-topsail yard would show in the water, there was at the very least 60 feet [18m] of the animal *á fleur d'eau*, no portion of which was, to our perception, used in propelling it through the water, either by vertical or horizontal undulation. It passed rapidly, but so close under our lee quarter, that had it been a man of my acquaintance, I should easily have recognized his features with the naked eye; and it did not, either in approaching the ship or after it had passed our wake, deviate in the slightest degree from its course to the S.W., which it held on at the pace of 12 to 25 miles per hour [20–40kph], apparently on some determined purpose.

'The diameter of the serpent was about 15 or 16 inches [38–41cm] behind the head, which was, without any doubt, that of a snake, and it was never, during the 20 minutes that it continued in sight of our glasses, once below the surface of the water; its colour a dark brown, with yellowish white about the throat. It had no fins, but something like the mane of a horse, or rather a bunch of seaweed, washed about its back. It was seen by the quartermaster, the boatswain's mate, and the man at the wheel, in addition to myself and officers above mentioned.'

The *Illustrated London News* embellished this account with pictures based on a sketch made at the time and further descriptions from witnesses. A great furore rose in the press. Despite coming under fierce attack, Captain M'Quhae stuck doggedly to his original account, insisting that what he had seen had not been a 'whale, a grampus, a great shark, an alligator, nor any of the larger surface-swimming creatures fallen in with

BELOW: *The 'Dædalus' sea serpent as published in The* Illustrated London News *in 1848.*

in ordinary voyages' as he was familiar with them all. He similarly dismissed the possibility that it could have been an elephant seal whose size he had misread, since as a naval captain he was well used to estimating lengths and distances accurately at sea.

The 'Daedalus' sea serpent is disappointing in that it was not threshing through the water in vertical loops, as in the classic image of the sea serpent; sceptics have even suggested that perhaps it was simply an abandoned canoe that had a carved prow and was being towed along by a harpooned shark or whale, invisible below the surface. Whatever the truth, the sighting was a milestone in the history of sea-serpent observation because of the debate and speculation it provoked, and the courage it gave other mariners to come out of the closet with their tales.

Moreover, for the first time it was proposed that the monster might be explained as a surviving example of the recently classified and supposedly extinct creature, the plesiosaur – that it was a living dinosaur. This has remained the most popular theory to account for sea and lake monsters ever since.

A problem with monster sightings is that they are generally not made by people qualified to evaluate what they see. When Captain M'Quhae swore that his creature had a head like a snake, he was just describing his impression. A naturalist would have looked harder, because the creature was not swimming in the way a snake would have, but, thanks to serendipity, some of the witnesses have been professionals.

One of the most interesting reports from the early 20th century was published in the *Proceedings of the Zoological Society* in 1906. It was written by two Fellows of the Society, E.G.B. Meade-Waldo and M.J. Nicoll, who swore they saw a sea serpent while on an expedition off the coast of Brazil. Meade-Waldo wrote that at 10.15am on 7 December 1905 Nicoll called his attention to something in the water about 100yd (90m) from their yacht, the *Valhalla*:

'I looked and immediately saw a large fin or frill sticking out of the water, dark seaweed brown in colour, somewhat crinkled at the edge. It was apparently about 6 feet [1.8m] in length and projected from 18 inches to 2 feet [46–60cm] from the water.

'I got my field glasses on to it … and almost as soon as I had them on the frill, a great head and neck rose out of the water in front of the frill; the neck did not touch the frill in the water, but came out of the water in front of it, at a distance of certainly not less than 18 inches [46cm], probably more. The neck appeared about the thickness of a slight man's body, and from 7 to 8 feet [2.1–2.4m] was out of the water; head and neck were all about the same thickness.'

Elsewhere Meade-Waldo added that the creature made a wave as it swam, and the two men saw a large body below the surface. It swung its neck from side to side, lashing the

ABOVE: *Another representation of the the 'Dædalus' sea serpent in* The Illustrated London News *in 1848.*

LEFT: *A drawing of the Valhalla's sea monster, based upon a sketch by an eye-witness, which appeared in The* Illustrated London News *in 1906.*

surface, and the head slightly resembled that of a turtle. Nicoll's version of events was much the same. Meade-Waldo and Nicoll were at a loss to explain the encounter, and undecided as to whether the creature was a reptile or a mammal, but they were prepared to stake their reputations that what they had seen was real.

Such accounts show that sea serpents are more than just children born from the fevered imaginations of vulnerable sailors long ago. Sailing the oceans in cockleshell craft no larger than known sea monsters like the whale was not just a heroic challenge to the physical elements but a defiance of all the demons that humans everywhere project onto the unknown. On land maps the legend 'Here Be Dragons' signified areas of which nothing was known; on marine charts the equivalent blanks were filled with monsters.

Seafarers today worry less about such encounters, of course, but that makes it all the more alarming when they do meet an unidentifiable monster – particularly if their craft is no more substantial than those of the Vikings or of St Brendan. During his row across the Atlantic in 1966 with Chay Blyth, Captain John Ridgeway was taking the midnight watch alone when the craft was almost overturned by what he could only describe as a sea serpent. Like Captain M'Quhae he was familiar with whales, sharks, dolphins, porpoises, flying fish and all the other creatures it might have been, but none of these fitted what he saw.

The important point about sea monsters is that they have not yet been completely dismissed as impossible. Leviathan and the Midgard Serpent may have been steadily edged into the realm of myth, but legends of terrifying sea monsters do still persist. Strange carcasses get washed ashore. The sea serpent's freshwater cousins – like Nessie, Nahuelito and Champ – tease us with continuing if fleeting appearances, reminding us that, if their lakes are wide, deep and little-explored, how much more so are the oceans. The Kraken has even gained a measure of scientific recognition, though the lifestyle of these purported creatures remains largely a matter of conjecture.

The oceans may still guard many secrets and shelter many strange forms of creation that act out their destinies happily indifferent to us.

1

Myth & Legend

Sea monsters are among the most basic creatures of legend for all seafaring nations. They incarnate the untameable elements that sailors have to wrestle with daily, the menace that hides beneath the waves and might pounce at any moment. The Scandinavians have given us some of the most vivid ones on all levels from high myth to real everyday peril, so it is fitting that we should open with the greatest sea monster of all, one that even the ocean could barely contain.

The Midgard Serpent

Jormungand, the Midgard Serpent, was one of three children fathered on the giantess Angrboda by Loki, the Norse god of mischief and trickery; the other two were Fenris the wolf and Hel, which means Death. When the gods learned of these offspring they remembered certain prophecies of the doom they would bring. So Odin the Allfather ordered they be brought to him so that he could decide their fate. Hel was given charge of the Underworld, Niflheim, to which go all those who suffer the humiliation of dying of old age or sickness instead of falling nobly in battle. Fenris the wolf was fostered by the gods, who tried to tame his savage nature. The Midgard Serpent was cast by Odin into the ocean, where she grew so huge that, with her tail in her mouth like an ouroboros, she soon came to encompass the whole world; the churnings of her coils raise the tsunami and tempests that drown sailors.

The thunder-god Thor had a particular hatred of the Midgard Serpent, and it began in this way. On one occasion he and a company of other gods, including Loki, went adventuring into Utgard, the land of the giants. They came to a vast castle whose gate even Thor could not push open; luckily it was so large they could squeeze in through the bars. The king of this castle and of the giants, Utgard-Loki (no relation to the god Loki), seemed unimpressed when he learned who his visitors were. He said he had expected the famous gods of Asgard to be somewhat more than midgets and that, if they wanted his hospitality, they would first have to perform some feat to impress him. He therefore challenged them to a series of seemingly minor tasks — at which they all failed.

The horn of the Midgard Serpent

One task set Thor was to lift up Utgard-Loki's grey cat, something which even the children of the castle could supposedly do. The best Thor could manage was to raise one of her paws a little off the floor. A famous drinker, Thor was next challenged to drain Utgard-Loki's drinking horn; despite his mightiest efforts the level barely fell below the rim. After this he became so furious with shame he wanted a fight, but Utgard-Loki said that, because Thor had performed so miserably before, the only contestant he could offer was his old nurse Elli. Thor, the champion of Asgard, was forced to accept this humiliation and began to wrestle with the old crone. But even at this he failed.

However, as it was late Utgard-Loki said the company of gods could stay the night despite having failed to prove their worth. The next morning they were given breakfast hospitably enough and shown on their way. When they were some distance from the castle, Utgard-Loki confessed the truth: the tasks had been more than they seemed, for he was a great enchanter. For example, the grey cat had in reality been the Midgard Serpent, whom Thor had nearly succeeded in wrenching from the ocean bed. The drinking horn had been connected to the ocean and Thor had noticeably drained the sea and created the first tides. And the crone was in fact old age, which no one can conquer.

When he heard all this, Thor was furious and turned to smash Utgard-Loki with his hammer, but the king of the giants had magically disappeared. Then Thor turned to

attack the castle, but it too had vanished. The thunder-god swore revenge there and then, not least on the Midgard Serpent, because at least he knew where she could be found.

Soon afterwards, travelling in the guise of a youth, Thor stayed the night with a giant called Hymir who lived by the sea. In the morning, as Hymir was preparing to go fishing, Thor asked if he could go too. The giant agreed – but reluctantly, as he said he could see little advantage in having such a stripling in his boat. When Thor asked what sort of bait he should bring, Hymir replied offhandedly that he should go and find his own bait.

So Thor went over to the largest of the giant's bulls, wrenched off its head and tossed this casually into the bottom of the boat. Then he took the oars and started rowing vigorously out to sea. Despite himself Hymir was impressed, and somewhat afraid. When they reached the spot where he usually fished, the giant told Thor to stop rowing; but the god ignored him and carried on out towards the edge of the world. Hymir pleaded with him to stop because, if they went much further, they might meet the Midgard Serpent. Ignoring him again, Thor rowed on until he felt sure they would find Jormungand and then fixed the bull's head to a great hook on a strong line and dropped it over the side.

By chance the serpent happened to be passing. She took the dainty morsel into her mouth but, when she felt the hook, jerked so hard that Thor was dragged to the gunwale. Summoning all his strength, he pulled back with such might that his feet burst through

Looking for trouble

the bottom of the boat. There followed a furious battle as Thor slowly hauled up the serpent until they were eye to glaring eye and it seemed as if a thunderstorm were raging between them.

Hymir was terrified by both the serpent and the water rushing into his boat and, as Thor raised his hammer to end the struggle, the giant quickly reached across and cut the hooked line. The serpent slithered gratefully back into the deep water. Thor desperately threw his hammer after her but was too late to prevent her escape. In fury the god turned and dealt Hymir such a blow that the giant fell overboard and was drowned.

Jormungand

Thereafter the Midgard Serpent, terrified by her close shave with Thor took care to hide in the depths of the sea where Thor might not find her; this is why she is now seen only rarely by humans. Although Thor swore to complete his revenge on the Midgard Serpent, he is not destined to do so until Ragnarok, the end of the world, when heaven, earth and the underworld will be destroyed. The Midgard Serpent will at that time rise from the bottom of the seabed to cause untold havoc and destruction. Thor will finally succeed in crushing the skull of his old enemy but will himself be slain in her dying struggles.

The Kraken

The other great sea monster of Norse myth and legend is the Kraken, said to be able to overturn ships and drag them down into the cold depths. There seems to be a degree of confusion with the Midgard Serpent, because some legends say there are only two Kraken in existence, and that these were born in the first creation and are destined to die only when the world itself finally perishes. This seems to be what Alfred Lord Tennyson (1809–1892) had in mind in his poem 'The Kraken' (1830):

Below the thunders of the upper deep;
Far, far beneath in the abysmal sea,
His ancient, dreamless, uninvaded sleep
The Kraken sleepeth: faintest sunlights flee
About his shadowy sides: above him swell
Huge sponges of millennial growth and height;
And far away into the sickly light,
From many a wondrous grot and secret cell
Unnumbered and enormous polypi
Winnow with giant arms the slumbering green.
There hath he lain for ages and will lie
Battening upon huge sea worms in his sleep,
Until the latter fire shall heat the deep;
Then once by man and angels to be seen,
In roaring he shall rise and on the surface die.

However, there are less apocalyptic tales about the Kraken – in particular about the 'young Kraken' – that contradict this, suggesting something on a lesser scale than the Midgard Serpent, though still scary enough. In the mid-18th century Erik Ludvigsen Pontoppidan (1698–1764), Bishop of Bergen, tackled the long and hazy tradition of the Kraken in his *Natural History of Norway* (1752–1753). After scrupulously interviewing mariners he came up with this remarkable tale, which repeated a tradition that can be traced back to the 12th century but is certainly much older.

Fishermen told Erik Pontoppidan that sometimes when they rowed several miles out to sea, particularly on hot, calm summer days, they found that in areas where they were used to sounding a depth of 80–100 fathoms (50–60m), they would find it registering less than half this. If the fish were also jumping, the fisherman guessed that the Kraken was lurking below, stirring them up. So, while keeping a careful watch on their depth-lines, the men would gratefully catch fish until the monster showed signs of rising to the surface. Then they would haul in their nets and paddle for their lives.

OPPOSITE:

The Kraken wakes

Once clear they would rest on their oars and, as Pontoppidan tells it, they would soon see an enormous monster rise to the surface — a creature so vast that no one could see the whole of it at once. The bishop says that it had the appearance of a number of small islands surrounded by something resembling seaweed:

'At last several bright points or horns appear, which grow thicker and thicker the higher they rise above the surface of the water, and sometimes they stand as high and large as the masts of middle-sized vessels. It seems these are the creature's arms and, it is said, if they were to lay hold of the largest man-of-war, they would pull it down to the bottom. After this monster has been on the surface of the water a short time, it begins slowly to sink again, and then the danger is as great as before, because the motion of this sinking causes such a swell in the sea, and such an eddy or whirlpool, that it draws down everything with it.'

This curiously symbiotic relationship with the Kraken is explained by Pontoppidan: 'The Kraken have never been known to do any great harm, except that they have taken away the lives of those who consequently could not bring the tidings.'

Presumably he meant there were legends of ships and sailors being attacked, but that this was rare and never occurred in the circumstances he describes above. He personally heard only one close anecdote: two unwary fishermen suddenly ran into a 'young Kraken', one of whose 'horns' or tentacles 'crushed the head of the boat, so that it was with great difficulty they saved their lives on the wreck, though the weather was as calm as possible'.

Writing as he was in the Age of Enlightenment, Pontoppidan was laughed to scorn by many naturalists who thought he had fallen for a bunch of fishermen's yarns. About the only part of his report taken seriously was his mention of the 'young Kraken'. This creature was well known to Norwegian fishermen; to judge by their descriptions, 'young Kraken' are quite clearly ordinary squid. But, although evidence was then emerging that squid could grow much larger than previously imagined, the suggestion that one might have a circumference of over a mile remained outrageous. Some rationalists suggested — as in other cases of supposed monsters surfacing at sea — that what the fishermen were talking about, in a garbled and fanciful way, was simply the surfacing of weed tangles, buoyed up by the gases of their own decomposition. But most people simply laughed the tales away.

Proof of a kind that Pontoppidan's sailors may not have been exaggerating came in a curious way during the Second World War. While hunting for German submarines off the coast of Norway, ships of the US Navy found a strange conundrum. Sometimes in areas where they knew the depth to be over 150 fathoms (90m) their sonar would indicate a much lower figure. Closer investigation showed that this phantom layer would rise gently towards the surface at night, then sink during the day. This suggested some kind of dense blanket of living organisms maintaining temperature by adjusting their depth.

The phenomenon is still unresolved but a reasonable suggestion is that it was probably caused by large schools of squid fanning out all at the same depth. And, if such a shoal surfaced, it might well appear, as Pontoppidan wrote, 'like a number of small islands, surrounded with something that floats and fluctuates like seaweeds'.

So is the Kraken in the end no more than a large school of squid breaking the surface? Well, possibly; but, as we shall discover later (see page 64), squid are continuing to surprise us by the size they can reach. One wonders, too, about the phantom submarines which both sides chased occasionally in Scandinavian waters during the Cold War. Perhaps squid may indeed reach a size still not fully appreciated by either science or the world in general, and thus be the true Kraken.

St Brendan's Voyage

The idea of floating islands which turn out to be living monsters was around long before Pontoppidan's day. It was first popularized in the original bestiary, often called the Physiologus after its purported author, compiled in Alexandria in the 3rd or 4th century and much augmented by later writers. This was the basis of most medieval bestiaries and its indiscriminate blend of fact, myth and fantasy helped colour the medieval European worldview almost as much as did the Bible, which it rivalled as a bestseller.

Unicorns, griffins, mermaids and a host of other fabulous creatures jostled elephants, apes, giraffes and the like, which to most readers seemed hardly more plausible, and which they were just as unlikely to meet in real life.

Tales from the *Physiologus* filtered east and west into a host of legends. In the *Arabian Nights* Sinbad colourfully tells how on his first voyage he came to an island that turned out to be a monster. This happened also to St Brendan and his monks according to the celebrated tale of their 6th-century Atlantic voyage which, among other things, has been read as suggesting that the Irish discovered the Americas before even the Vikings. According to the story, St Brendan found a glut of strange islands out in the Atlantic, none stranger than this one, recounted in *The Navigation of St Brendan* (c1050):

'Their vessel ran aground and the monks, on their master's advice, stepped out into the shallows and tied ropes to either side of the boat so they could drag it ashore. The island was rocky and bare. There was hardly a grain of sand on the beach and just an occasional tree here and there. The monks landed and passed the whole night in prayer in the open. Brendan stayed aboard. He knew perfectly what kind of island it was but kept from telling the others in case they took fright.

'In the morning he told those monks who were priests to say Mass, which they did. Then the monks took from their vessel joints of raw meat and fish which they had brought with them, and sprinkled them with salt. Then they lit a fire and put a cooking pot on it. But when the pot began to boil, the island started to heave like a wave. The monks ran to the boat, begging their abbot to protect them. He dragged them in one by one and they set off, leaving behind everything they had taken ashore. The island moved away over the sea and from two miles

Jasconius

and more the monks could still see their fire burning brightly. Brendan asked: "Brethren, does the island's behaviour surprise you?"

"We are almost petrified with fright," they replied.

"Have no fear, my sons. Last night God revealed the meaning of this wonder in a dream. It was no island that we landed on, but that animal which is the greatest of all creatures that swim in the sea. It is called Jasconius." '

But whether by this name (which is simply derived from *iasc*, the Irish for 'fish') Brendan meant Leviathan, the Midgard Serpent, the Kraken or something totally different is left for us to guess.

Quetzalcoatl

The name means Feathered (or Plumed) Serpent, and this is how Quetzalcoatl is most often portrayed. The quetzal bird, from which the god took his title and plumage, belongs to the Trogon family; its body is the size of a magpie's but the male's gorgeous tail feathers can grow up to 3ft (1m) long. It feeds mainly on fruit, and thus would have been a common visitor to the god's famous orchards.

Quetzalcoatl had various areas of responsibility but, as a divine serpent he was, like the lake-dwelling dragons of China and the Indian nagas, a rain god and hence a patron of fertility. But, being a supreme divinity, he could adopt other guises, being associated also with thunder, wind and fire. These elements had in addition their own individual deities, who were often at war with each other. By combining all the elements in himself Quetzalcoatl, the creator of life and civilization, declared his primacy. Unlike most Central and South American deities, he was opposed to war and, in general, human sacrifice, being kind and benevolent and preaching simplicity and virtue. He was associated with Venus, the Morning Star.

Quetzalcoatl

Atlantis sinking

In human form Quetzalcoatl is commonly shown as a pale-skinned, bearded man wearing a conical cap; when not dressed in a shamanistic serpent costume he often wears a long robe decorated with crosses. As ruler of Mexico he is said to have introduced metallurgy, agriculture, good government and all the other arts. His reign was a golden age of peace, plenty and justice. He introduced the calendar and lived an ascetic life, being both celibate and teetotal. In place of human sacrifice he taught his people to offer the gods tributes of bread, flowers, incense and prayers. The only blood sacrifice he encouraged was voluntary self-sacrifice – the letting of one's own blood or 'jewel water' as a free offering. From time to time he sailed eastward across the Atlantic to his birthplace for a while. He was finally defeated and driven out by his great rival and enemy Tezcatlipoca, the sun god, who demanded human sacrifices in return for withholding drought.

When he recognized defeat, Quetzalcoatl burned his houses. He turned his attendants into brightly coloured birds to accompany him, and set sail across the eastern ocean in a ship made of serpents (or perhaps one shaped like a serpent). In departing he said to those left behind that he would one day return. Or, as one version says, he told them that 'there should surely come to them in after times, by way of the sea where the sun rises, certain white men with beards like him, and that these would be his brothers and rule that land'.

The Spanish adventurer Hernando Cortés (1485–1547), with his pale skin and shining armour, happened to land at what is now called Vera Cruz, the place from which Quetzalcoatl had departed, and was mistaken for the returning god by coastguards serving the Aztec emperor, Montezuma II (1466–1520). This misidentification was largely responsible for the ensuing collapse of the indigenous civilization.

The Conquistadors were impressed to find the cross in common use in Central America as a religious symbol; one of the first Mexican treasures sent by Cortés to the King of Spain was even described in the inventory as 'a cross with a crucifix and its support'. This persuaded the Spanish that some Christian apostle must have brought the Good News to America long before.

It is wonderful how much natural confusion was built into the clash of cultures. The Spanish looked for Christianity while the Mexicans thought their old god had returned, possibly in a vengeful mood. Topiltzin Quetzalcoatl was the focus of the confusion. Some Spanish missionaries read in his tale a distorted memory of the apostle Thomas, who had last been seen sailing off into the sunset looking for converts. A connection is that Thomas bore the sobriquet Didymus, meaning 'the Twin', and Quetzalcoatl's name can be rendered as 'Precious Twin'.

Other theorists went even further and suggested that Quetzalcoatl might be Jesus himself. The parallels were suggestive. Quetzalcoatl was said in Mexican myth (or so it was interpreted) to be the only son of the supreme deity, Tonacatecutle, also called Citinatonali, which means 'god of heaven'. His mother was Chimalman, the Virgin of Tula, who was impregnated by the god's mere breath. Quetzalcoatl was said to be both god (serpent) and man; he freely chose to be incarnated in order to bring reason and mercy to the world. He was even supposed in some accounts to have been crucified, but this was probably confusion and/or wishful thinking on the part of the missionaries.

In the late 19th century it became popular to tie the legend of Quetzalcoatl in with that of Atlantis, which still represented a fairly respectable field of speculation. Quetzalcoatl had come from Atlantis, it was said, and returned there after his defeat at the hands of the sun god; he had deployed Atlantean wisdom and technology in civilizing the Americas. Plato (c428–cc348bc), in his famous account of Atlantis in the *Timaeus* says:

'Beyond the strait where you place the Pillars of Hercules there was an island larger than Asia [Minor] and Libya combined. From this island one could pass easily to the other islands and from these to the continent which lies around the interior sea.'

Plato goes on to describe how a great army from Atlantis invaded and conquered the Mediterranean, until defeated by the early Athenians:

'Their defeat stopped the invasion and gave entire independence to all countries on this side of the Pillars of Hercules. Afterwards, in one day and one fatal night, there came mighty earthquakes and inundations, which engulfed that warlike people; Atlantis disappeared beneath the sea, and then that sea became inaccessible, so that navigation on it ceased on account of the quantity of mud which the engulfed island left in its place.'

Although Plato here and in the later, unfinished *Critias* goes into great detail about the geography, history and culture of Atlantis, most people accepted even in the 19th century that he had made much of it up, his purpose being fabular. But nevertheless there has always been a lingering suspicion that Plato merely exaggerated a real tradition. He — or at least *Critias*, which was his mouthpiece in the relevant dialogues — laid great emphasis on it being a true tale. This is also supported by other scattered and teasing allusions elsewhere in the classical literature to Phoenicians and Egyptians trading, during Old Testament times, with some rich continent west of the Pillars of Hercules.

OPPOSITE:

Guardian of the ruins

Leviathan

The Biblical sea monster, Leviathan, is a tantalizingly vague figure, at least within the accepted canon of biblical books. Although often enough used as a metaphor in sermons and homilies, the exact nature of the beast is confused.

Leviathan's lair

It is generally assumed that Leviathan was a whale, certainly Captain Ahab thought so in *Moby Dick*, but that does not really fit descriptions in the Bible. Also the whale is several times mentioned in the Bible as simply a whale, (though the whale that swallowed Jonah is referred to as a big fish). The clearest description of Leviathan in the Bible comes from the famous passage in the *Book of Job* where God rather unkindly taunts poor Job for his powerlessness:

'Canst thou draw out Leviathan with an hook? Or his tongue with a cord which thou lettest down? Canst thou put an hook into his nose? Or bore his jaw through with a

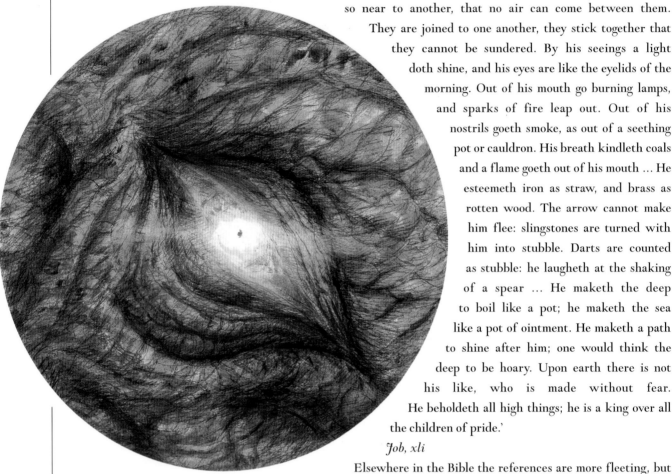

thorn? ... I will not conceal his parts, nor his power, nor his comely proportion. Who can discover the face of his garment? Or who can come to him with his double bridle? Who can open the doors of his face? His teeth are terrible round about. His scales are his pride, shut up together as with a close seal. One is so near to another, that no air can come between them. They are joined to one another, they stick together that they cannot be sundered. By his seeings a light doth shine, and his eyes are like the eyelids of the morning. Out of his mouth go burning lamps, and sparks of fire leap out. Out of his nostrils goeth smoke, as out of a seething pot or cauldron. His breath kindleth coals and a flame goeth out of his mouth ... He esteemeth iron as straw, and brass as rotten wood. The arrow cannot make him flee: slingstones are turned with him into stubble. Darts are counted as stubble: he laugheth at the shaking of a spear ... He maketh the deep to boil like a pot; he maketh the sea like a pot of ointment. He maketh a path to shine after him; one would think the deep to be hoary. Upon earth there is not his like, who is made without fear. He beholdeth all high things; he is a king over all the children of pride.'

Job, xli

Elsewhere in the Bible the references are more fleeting, but still suggest something other than a whale:

'In that day the Lord with his sore and great and strong sword shall punish Leviathan the piercing serpent, even Leviathan that crooked serpent; and he shall slay the dragon that is in the sea.'

Isaiah, xxvii 1

'O Lord how manifold are thy works! In wisdom hast thou made them all; the earth is full of thy riches. So is this great and wide sea, wherein are things creeping innumerable, both small and great beasts. There go the ships; there is that Leviathan, whom thou hast made to play therein.'

Psalms, civ 24–6

Jewish legend has more to say. The *Talmud* tells us that Leviathan is so large it has to eat a fish three miles (5km) long every day to satisfy its hunger. Elsewhere there is a legend that soon after the Creation, God realized the pair of Leviathans He had created were likely to devour everything in the sea if they were allowed to breed. So He killed one and made the other immortal, thereby preserving at least part of His original grand design.

Some Christians also connect Leviathan with the great dragon in the *Book of Revelation*, thus giving the beast a rather similar apocalyptic role to that of the Midgard Serpent.

The eye of Leviathan
'by his seeing a light
doth shine'

Scylla and Charybdis

In The Odyssey *Homer (8th century bc) tells how his
hero, Odysseus is at one point warned by the goddess Circe that
he will have to sail through a narrow and dreadful channel
between two peaks. Halfway up a cliff in the taller one,
beyond bowshot, is a cave where lives Scylla,whose awful
bark sounds no more than the call of a newborn pup, but
who is a dreadful monster whom not even a god can
look upon without a shudder.*

Scylla

'She has twelve feet dangling in the air and six long necks, each ending in a grisly head, with triple rows of teeth set thick and close, blackly charged with death. Up to her middle she is sunk in the depths of the cave, but sways her heads out across the dizzy abyss. Thus she fishes without leaving her cave, catching dolphins or swordfish or any of the larger creatures that dwell in the roaring seas. No crew can ever boast that they sailed their ship past Scylla without loss, since from every passing vessel she snatches a man with each of her heads, and so carries off her prey.'

Charybdis

Odysseus's problem, however, is that below the other rock is an even worse menace, the dreaded whirlpool known as Charybdis:

'Three times a day she spews the waters up, and three times a day she swallows them down again. Heaven keep you from getting too near, for then not even the Earthshaker could save you.'

So the choice before Odysseus is stark: either he must lose his whole ship down Charybdis's gullet or just six of the crew to Scylla. He asks if perhaps they can fight Scylla but Circe replies:

'Scylla was not born for death: the fiend will live forever. She is a thing to shun, intractable, ferocious and impossible to fight. Against her there is no defence. If you waste time trying to fight her, I only fear she may dart out once more with all six heads and snatch another six of your men. So just drive your ship past with all your might.'

Reluctantly Odysseus accepts this, and sets sail for the place without telling his men of the dreadful dilemma. When they come in sight of the whirlpool he still says nothing beyond telling them to steer as far away as possible.

Charybdis is even worse than Odysseus has expected. In his words:

'When she vomited up the waters, she was stirred to her depths and seethed like a cauldron on a blazing fire; and the spray she flung on high rained down on the tops of the crags at either side. But when she swallowed the salt water down, the whole interior of her vortex was exposed, the rocks re-echoed to her fearful roar and the dark sands of the sea bottom came into view.'

Transfixed by this dreadful sight, the crew notice only too late that six of their number have been snatched high into the air. Odysseus in retrospect says:

'For like an angler on a jutting point, who with a long rod casts his ox-horn lure into the sea as bait for the little fish below, gets a bite and whips his struggling prize to land, Scylla had whisked my comrades up and swept them struggling to the rocks where she devoured them at her own door, shrieking and stretching out their hands to me in their last desperate throes. In all I have gone through as I made my way across the seas, I have never had to witness a more pitiable sight than that.'

MYTH & LEGEND

Hydra

Another great monster of ancient Greek legend was the Hydra, or Water-Snake, which is said to have lived in a swamp near Lerna, in the country of Argos. Its breath and blood were deadly poisonous and it jealously guarded a spring and stream, which had been created with Neptune's trident by the nymph, Amymone, to relieve the country of drought.

The Hydra was most commonly said to have nine heads, one of which was immortal and impossible to destroy. But the number of heads varied because the monster's peculiar talent was that each time one was cut off, two more grew in its place. Illustrated on the opposite page is the moment before the first unlucky hero discovers this terrifying aspect of the Hydra.

The Hydra terrorized the countryside around Lerna for years and disposed of all challengers. Then along came Hercules wearing his lion skin and with his club over his shoulder. He was riding a chariot driven by his faithful nephew, Iolaus, who shared many of his adventures. They had been sent by King Eurystheus of Mycenae, who was afraid that Hercules might one day steal his crown. With the goddess Hera's aid, he tricked Hercules into accepting ten challenges, partly just to keep him away from home, partly in the hope that one or the other of the adventures would prove too much for him and he would not return at all.

The first was to take on a mighty lion that had been terrorizing the valley of Nemea. When his club and arrows proved useless, Hercules strangled the lion with his bare hands and carried it back to his king on his shoulders.

Eurystheus was impressed but also more nervous than ever, so he next ordered Hercules to go and kill the so-far invincible Hydra. Arriving at its lair by the spring, Hercules flushed the monster out by shooting flaming arrows into the cave. Then he ran upon it with his club and began knocking off the nine heads. But of course each time he did so, two more appeared, so things were soon much worse than in the beginning. Nor could Hercules retreat because the Hydra had coiled itself firmly around his legs. On top of which a giant crab that lived with the Hydra now came and joined in the fray. Well, the crab wasn't immortal and was soon turned to paste, but the Hydra was now becoming a serious menace.

Hercules called out for help and, with sudden inspiration, Iolaus set fire to a grove of trees, then joined the battle brandishing flaming branches and cauterizing the wound each time Hercules knocked off a head, so that it could not grow again. Finally, the Hydra's last immortal head was knocked off and buried under a huge boulder beside the road from Lerna to Elaeus. Then Hercules cut open the Hydra's body and dipped the tips of his arrows in its venomous ichor, and these poisoned arrows were later to prove very useful in his adventures.

Sadly, though, Eurystheus refused to accept that Hercules had fulfilled his task because of Iolaus' help, and promptly set him another. In this way the original ten challenges Hercules had agreed to became his famous Twelve Labours, which he completed in as many years.

Hydra

A Mermaid Tale

Mermaids are hardly monsters in the sense in which we generally use the term, but it would be a pity to omit mention of them altogether. What is not generally realized is that, until as recently as about the 18th century, they were in Europe widely believed to be real. Some noble families even claimed descent from them, such as the houses of Luxembourg, Rohan and Sassanaye.

OPPOSITE:

Merpeople

From France comes the legend of Melusina, a maiden with whom Raymond Duke of Poitiers fell in love. She agreed to marry him on condition that she could have one day a week of privacy. All went well until one day curiosity got the better of him. He spied on her taking a bath and to his horror found he had married a mermaid who was from the navel downwards 'in likeness of a great serpent'. When she realized her secret was out, Melusina vanished, but her image was incorporated into Raymond's family coat of arms.

2

SEA SERPENTS

All fishermen of Norway are agreed that there is a Sea Serpent 200 feet [60m] long and 20 feet [6m] thick that lives in caves and rocks near Bergen ... He hath commonly hair hanging from his neck a cubit [46–56cm] long, sharp scales, and is black and hath flaming, shining eyes. He puts his head up on high like a pillar.

Erik Pontoppidan, *Natural History of Norway (1752–1753)*

Pontoppidan's sea monster

Reliable sightings of sea serpents are far more common than most people think. For his cryptozoological classic *In the Wake of the Sea Serpents* (1965) Bernard Heuvelmans collected reports of over 500 clearly documented sightings from the previous two centuries. Most of the beasts were observed by more than one witness, some by over 100. He also studied hundreds of more vague accounts. For each sighting that he recorded one can safely say there are many he did not discover – apart from any other reason, claiming to have seen a sea serpent has blighted many lives, so witnesses may advisedly think twice before reporting what they have seen.

'Sea serpent' is the term that comes to mind whenever people see a large unknown monster in the ocean. The term has probably been applied to many different creatures but, as with lake monsters, most described sea serpents fall into two main categories: what we might call the 'true' sea serpents, many-humped, serpentine

creatures which appear to move with vertical coils; and plesiosaur-like monsters with a large body and a long, slender neck. Often, of course, it is not clear which of the two kinds has been seen: a sighting of a plesiosaur might be interpreted by witnesses as of a 'true' sea serpent, and vice versa, much depending on the prejudices of the viewer. So, for convenience, the two categories are lumped together. Sightings are, as Scandinavian sailors have always maintained, commonest in calm weather.

The estimated lengths of sea serpents vary from 20ft to 250ft (6 to 75m), but most guesses fall in the middle range, suggesting an average length of 150ft (46m). In fact, in terms of body-mass this is not particularly large for a marine creature: length for length, a sea serpent would weigh much less than a whale. The largest whale on record was 113ft (35m) long and weighed over 150 tons. A sea serpent of the same weight would be about 250ft (75m) in length.

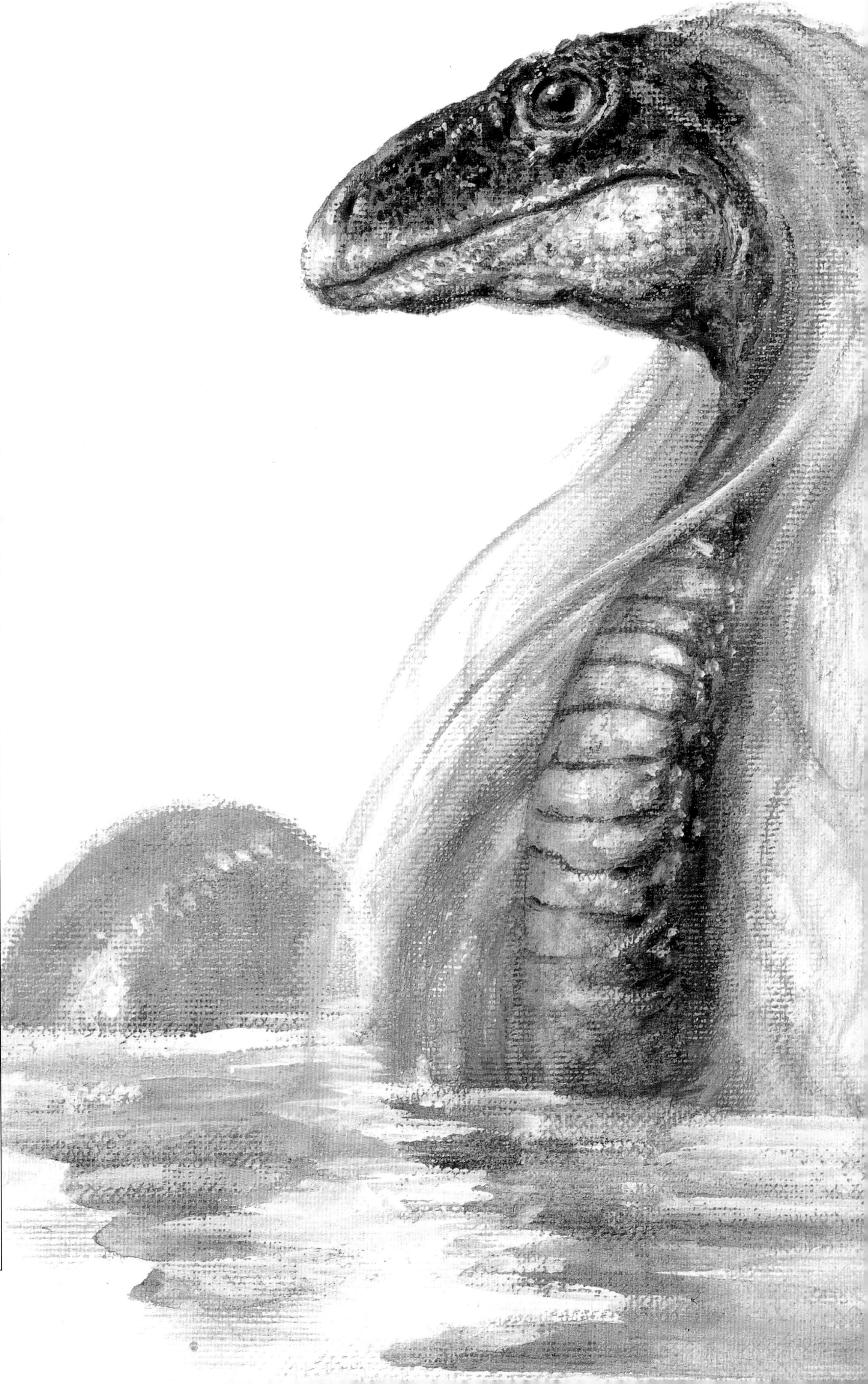

The Romsdalfiord Serpent

For a long time it seemed as if only Scandinavian sailors met sea serpents, so elsewhere the creatures were widely dismissed as a Norse delusion. Bishop Pontoppidan himself was sceptical until persuaded by the certainty with which his witnesses gave their accounts — to Bergen fishermen his doubts seemed as odd as if he were questioning the existence of eels or cod.

A typical sighting from Pontoppidan's time and included in his *Natural History of Norway* (1752–1753) is that of Lorenz von Ferry, a 'Royal Commander and Pilot General' with the Norwegian Navy. It was presented as a sworn

OPPOSITE:

The Romsdalfiord serpent

statement in public court in Bergen five years after the event. Backed by his crew and other witnesses, von Ferry declared that one calm, hot day at the end of August 1746 he was being rowed towards Molde in the province of Romsdal in Norway, reading a book as his men strained at the oars, when he noticed them muttering in alarm and slacking off. The problem, he was told, was that there was a sea serpent blocking their way – as indeed he found to be the case. Like a true Viking, Captain von Ferry ordered his reluctant crew to give chase. When the serpent looked

like getting away he took out his gun, which happened to be loaded, and shot it. The creature dived, leaving a trail of blood on the surface. The captain's description, having come within a few yards of it, was: 'The head of this sea-serpent, which it held more than two feet [0.6m] above the surface of the water, resembled that of a horse. It was of a greyish colour, and the mouth was quite black and very large. It had large black eyes and a long white mane that hung down from the neck to the surface of the water. Besides the head and neck, we saw seven or eight folds or coils of this snake, which were very thick and, as far as we could guess, there was a fathom's distance between each fold.'

This creature was witnessed by several people ashore, and their statements confirmed the description in most of the details. Some observers also noticed small fins or limbs on the creature's sides.

A century later, in 1847, the London

Zoologist magazine, a great forum for the sea-serpent debate, published an account of a similar sighting off the Romsdal coast on 28 July 1845; of the four witnesses, two were pillars of the local community. It was a bright day and the sea was calm.

'About seven o'clock in the afternoon, a little distance from shore, near the ballast place and Molde Hooe, they saw a long marine animal, which slowly moved itself forward, as it appeared to them, with the help of two fins on the fore-part of the body nearest the head, which they judged from the boiling of the water on both sides of it.

'The visible part of the body appeared to be between forty and fifty feet [12–15m] in length, and moved in undulations like a snake. The body was round and of a dark colour, and seemed to be several ells in thickness. As they discerned a waving motion in the water behind the animal, they concluded that part of the body was concealed under water. That it was one connected animal they saw plainly from its movement. When the animal was about one hundred yards [90m] from the boat, they noticed tolerably correctly its fore-part, which ended in a sharp snout; its colossal head raised itself above the water in the form of a semi-circle; the lower part was not visible. The colour of the head was dark brown and the skin smooth. They did not notice the eyes or any mane or bristles on the throat.'

When the beast came within about 50yd (46m) they fired their guns and it dived. But, unlike von Ferry's serpent, it surfaced again.

'He raised his neck in the air like a snake preparing to dart on its prey. After he had turned and got his body in a straight line, which he appeared to do with great difficulty, he darted like an arrow against the boat. They reached the shore, and the animal perceiving it had come into shallow water, dived immediately and disappeared in the deep.'

From the late 18th century onwards North Americans discovered sea serpents on their own doorstep. There had always been sporadic reports, but these had attracted no great attention; now came dozens and even hundreds of sightings.

The most famous case was the creature of Gloucester Bay, Massachusetts. In summer 1817 it became such a common sight that a local justice of the peace collected affidavits from the more 'respectable' witnesses and presented them to the Linnean Society of New England for scientific scrutiny. The serpent seemed unafraid of humans, not objecting even when some took pot-shots at it. It became distinctly less bold after a harpoon attack in July 1818, but still continued to be seen by hundreds of people in the general area for about a further decade. A committee headed by Dr Hamilton summarized:

'The affidavits of a great many individuals of unblemished character are collected, which leaves no room to apprehend anything like deceit. They do not agree in every minute particular, but in regard to its great length and snake-like form, they are harmonious.'

An affidavit from Matthew Gaffney, an early witness, said that in the late afternoon of 14 August 1817 he saw:

'a strange marine animal, resembling a serpent, in the harbour in said Gloucester. I was in a boat, and was within thirty feet [9m] of him. His head appeared full as large as a four-gallon keg, his body as large as a barrel, and his length that I saw, I should judge forty feet [12m], at least. The top of his head was of a dark colour, and the under part of his head appeared nearly white, as did also several feet of his belly that I saw.'

In the spirit of his age, Gaffney then raised his rifle and shot at the creature's head. It turned towards the boat, not obviously harmed, and the sailors thought it was about to attack them. Instead it dived and swam under their boat, surfacing about 100yd (90m) away:

'He did not turn down like a fish, but appeared to settle directly down, like a rock ... His motion [undulation] was vertical, like a caterpillar.'

This apparent 'vertical undulation' was stressed in the affidavits, the witnesses being specifically asked whether the motion was vertical or horizontal. Another description, by the Reverend Cheever Felch, was published in the *Boston Sentinel*. He and several others had seen the beast at very close quarters from a dinghy belonging to the schooner *Science* in Gloucester Harbour on the morning of 26 August 1819:

'From my knowledge of aquatic animals, and habits of intimacy with marine appearances, I could not be deceived. We had a good view of him, except the very short period when he was under water, for half an hour. His colour is a dark brown, with white under the throat. His size we could not accurately ascertain, but his head is about three feet [0.9m] in circumference, flat and much smaller than his body. We did not see his tail; but from the end of his head to the fartherest protuberance, was not far from one hundred feet [30m]. I speak with a degree of certainty, from being much accustomed to measure and estimate distances and length. I counted fourteen bunches on his back; the first one, say ten or twelve feet [3–4m] from his head, and the others about seven feet [2m] apart. They decreased in size towards the tail. These bunches were sometimes counted with, and sometimes without a glass ... His motion was sometimes very rapid, and at other times he lay nearly still. He turned slowly, and took up considerable room in doing it. He sometimes darted under water, with the greatest velocity, as if seizing prey.'

Almost everyone in the Gloucester Bay area seems to have seen the beast during the weeks it remained during the summer of 1817, and there was broad agreement about its size and appearance; then it was spotted moving away along the coast. Sadly, the Linnaean Society's investigation ended in farce when the committee concluded that a small diseased land-snake presented to it must be the serpent's offspring.

For a while after the Gloucester Bay affair there were many reports of sea serpents all along the New England coast. Some were plainly hoaxes, but others did not deserve the mockery they received. The descriptions broadly tally with each other and with older tales from the other side of the Atlantic, the main difference being that Scandinavian reports often tell of a mane on the beast whereas this is hardly ever mentioned in those from North America's eastern seaboard.

A typical example of the plesiosaur type of sea serpent is one described by Captain R.J. Cringle in 1893. He was steaming in the ship *Umfuli* off Mauritania when it encountered a monster:

'When we first saw it, I estimated that it would be about 400 yards [370m] away. It was rushing through the water at great speed, and was throwing water from its breast as a vessel throws water from its bows. I saw full 15ft [4.6m] of its head and neck on three several occasions. The body was all the time visible ... The base, or body, from which the neck sprang, was much thicker than the neck itself, and I should not therefore call it a serpent. Had it been breezy enough to ruffle the water, or hazy, I should have had some doubt about the creature; but the sea being so perfectly smooth, I had not the slightest doubt in my mind as to its being a sea monster ... This thing, whatever it was, was in sight for over an hour. In fact we did not lose sight of it until darkness came on.'

OPPOSITE:

The Gloucester sea serpent

Cringle commented later that he wished he had never laid eyes on the thing because of the ridicule that was heaped on his head:

'I have been told that it was a string of porpoises, that it was an island of seaweed, I do not know what besides. But if an island of seaweed can travel at the rate of fourteen knots [26kph], or if a string of porpoises can stand 15ft [4.6m] out of the water, then I give in and confess myself deceived. Such, however, could not be.'

The 'Dædalus' serpent

Fear of similar ridicule kept Charles Seibert quiet for 46 years. He was encouraged to break silence by an article on sea monsters in the *Saturday Evening Post*. Seibert wrote in to say that in 1901 he had been aboard the steamer *Grangense* steaming from New York to Belem when he and others saw a sea monster nearby.

'It was some sort of amphibian, grayish brown in colour. The forward part, which was all we could see, was similar to the monster pictured in the *Post* [a plesiosaur-type creature]; however, its neck was not so thick or long. Its head was a trifle longer, more like a crocodile's. When it opened its mouth we could see rows of regular teeth, maybe four to six inches [10–15cm] long. It appeared to be playing on the surface, and would swirl in circles, bending its neck until it looked towards its tail, if it had one. It would gambol for maybe half a minute, then dive. This it did three times. We asked the captain if he was going to log the encounter. His reply was, "No fear. They will say we are all drunk, and I'll thank you mister, not to mention it to our agents at Para or Manaus." '

Others have seen monsters resembling crocodiles but in the deep ocean, and some of these creatures may even have been saltwater crocodiles, which can easily grow to 20ft (6m) and have sometimes been met far from shore in the western Pacific. They have even reached Fiji, some 500 miles (800km) from their nearest known normal habitat (they are estuary-dwellers); but they are unlikely to have travelled all the way to the Atlantic, where some 'crocodile-like' monsters have been seen.

Perhaps the most dramatic account comes from the German submarine *U28*. On 30 July 1915 it torpedoed the 5,000-ton British steamer *Iberian* in the open sea southwest of

Ireland. The *Iberian* sank quickly. This is how the U-boat's captain, Freiherr von Forstner, in a newspaper report some years later described what followed:

'The ship, which was about 180 metres [600ft] long, sank rapidly stern-first, the depth at this point being a few thousand metres. When the steamer had disappeared for about 25 seconds it exploded ... Shortly afterwards pieces of wreckage, among them a huge marine animal, writhing and struggling wildly, were shot out of the water to a height of 20 to 30 metres [70–100ft]. At this moment we were six men on the bridge... We at once centred our attention upon this wonder of the seas. Unfortunately we had not time to take a photograph because the animal disappeared after 10 or 15 seconds. It was about 20 metres [65ft] long, looked like a giant crocodile, and had four powerful paddle-like limbs and a long pointed head.'

Such descriptions are fairly common, so what we are possibly dealing with is a third main type of unclassified sea monster. It has been suggested it might be a surviving mosaosaur or thalattosuchian; these ancestors of the crocodile are otherwise believed to have died out with the bulk of dinosaurs 65 million years ago. It is worth mentioning that crocodiles themselves have changed little since that period; why these reptiles survived while their fairly close relatives, the dinosaurs, were extinguished is not known.

We might expect sea-serpent sightings to have tailed off when sails gave way to noisy steam and diesel engines, particularly as powered vessels stick to much narrower sea lanes, but they continued steadily into the 20th century and with as many plausible witnesses as before.

On 30 December 1947 the Greek ship *Santa Clara* found itself unable to avoid a large unidentified creature while sailing from New York to Columbia. In the collision the ship was, though badly shaken, undamaged, but the monster was mortally wounded, being apparently sliced in two. This happened on a clear calm day about 100 miles [165km] off Lookout Cape, North Carolina, and the crew had time to observe closely what followed. Captain John Fordan's account said that, soon after the collision, they saw a snake-like head appear above the surface about 10yd (9m) from the ship:

'The monster's head was about 30 inches [80cm] in breadth, 2 feet [60cm] thick and 4–5 feet [1.2–1.5m] long. The body was cylindrical, and about 3 feet [90cm] thick. When the creature was abreast of the Captain's bridge, they could see that the water was red over a radius of about 30–40 feet [10–12m]. The visible part of the body was about 34–36 feet [11m] long ... Its skin appeared to be dark brown, and smooth. No fins or hair nor protuberances were seen on its head or neck or other visible parts of the body.'

Another member of the crew described it as:

'a very large animal from which blood in enormous amounts was pouring into the wash. About 30 feet [9m] of its spindle-shaped, glistening body was above water, and this tapered at one end into a narrow but not too long neck on which was an enormous tapering triangular head stated by all witnesses to have been at least 3 feet [90cm] across above the eyes. The creature passed astern and was sucked into the wake where it thrashed about amid blood-red foam, until it finally sank. The ship stopped but nothing further was seen.'

It has been suggested that the creature may have been a giant eel; such eels may indeed exist, but the detailed descriptions of the head make the identification unlikely in this case. Eels generally have no visible neck, the head seeming to be directly joined to the body as in fishes. The crew of the *Santa Clara* must have known this; had the creature looked like a giant eel they would almost certainly have said so.

The sea serpent is so often described as moving with a 'vertical undulation' that this attribute cannot be ignored, although the immediate problem is that we should not then describe them as serpents. True serpents or snakes undulate horizontally: their backbones are unable to flex in any other way. So, while the sea serpent may look like a snake to a lay eye, if it undulates up and down as it swims it must be something else.

The anaconda python of Brazil, *Eunectes murinus*, is reasonably believed to grow up to 100ft (30m) in length, as is the African rock python, *Python sebae*. Both like water and are known to swim far out to sea – the first creature to reach Krakatoa after the eruption in 1883 is said to have been a large reticulated python, which must have swum at least 30 miles (50km) to get there. However, as noted, snakes swim with a very obvious horizontal motion that does not throw 'humps' or coils above the surface.

There are also the true sea-snakes, species of the zoological family Hydrophiidae, and these are known to grow up to 10ft (3m) long; those of the species *Hydrophis* have a pronounced neck and tail and a relatively plump body, so that they look like a flipperless plesiosaur. It is possible that specimens could grow longer than 10ft (3m), but this would not qualify them as putative sea serpents because, like terrestrial snakes, they swim with a horizontal wriggle. The same applies to giant eels and oarfish. Even so, such creatures probably do account for many supposed sea-serpent sightings. They cannot, however, be cited to explain the classic profile of the many-humped sea serpent. If the humps are not bumps or fins on the back of some creature – a monstrous sturgeon, for example – if they are the undulations of a serpentine beast, the explanation must lie elsewhere.

Whatever its true nature, something resembling a giant serpent but undulating vertically has been seen by sailors for hundreds of years. Most of the tales come from the North Atlantic, but many further plausible accounts come from every part of the globe. The list is almost endless. In fact, as Heuvelmans has pointed out, there are more recorded sightings of sea serpents than of many other perfectly accepted large denizens of the deep, such as devilfish, whale-sharks and beaked whales. It is therefore not all that far-fetched to suppose that the sea serpent is a real but as yet unclassified creature (or several different kinds of creature) that has possibly survived since the age of the dinosaurs.

Sea-serpent believers take comfort from the recent discovery of two other 'living

A shy sea serpent

fossils' in the ocean depths. One is the false killer whale, *Pseudorca crassidens*. This was believed to be long extinct until the turn of the 20th century, when several shoals were washed up on the Scottish coast. Similarly – but more spectacularly in terms of geological time – the coelacanth, an ugly fish with four stubby fins that resemble legs, was thought to have died out with the dinosaurs. Until 1938 no one thought to ask the fishermen of the Comoro Islands about this: they regularly catch coelacanths on their deep-water lines.

A remarkable thing about the coelacanth is that there is no fossil evidence of it after 70 million years ago; people who argue against other 'living fossils', such as the plesiosaur, should remind themselves of this. And those who still doubt the existence of large unknown sea creatures should remember that until November 1976 when a specimen was hauled from the sea near Hawaii the world was completely ignorant of one of the largest sharks – *Megachasma pelagios*, weighing up to a ton and popularly called 'megamouth'.

Chessie

Chesapeake Bay – the narrow arm of the Atlantic that reaches into North America towards Baltimore and Washington DC – has long been rumoured to have a resident sea serpent; some suggest the creature migrated south from New England, where similar sightings were recorded regularly until they petered out in the 19th century. 'Chessie fever' rose to a pitch in the 1970s, when the sobriquet was coined by the Richmond Times Gazette, *obviously with a nod to the creature's famous cousin in Scotland's Loch Ness.*

Sightings seem to coincide with the presence of shoals of bluefin, which visit the bay during summer. Descriptions very strongly suggest a serpentine creature, and it has been proposed that Chessie may be an anaconda, somehow brought by the ships which regularly trade to the area from South America. This is possible, but many witnesses speak of 'vertical undulations', so the proposition must remain in limbo until a specimen is brought ashore.

The Enigma Project, founded by Michael Frizzell and Robert Lazzara, has logged dozens, even hundreds of sightings of Chessie since the 1970s, and many of these are hard to doubt. To take an example, there was the occasion in September 1980 when Chessie was seen near Smith Point by no fewer than about 25 passengers aboard four separate charter boats. The captain of one boat told the *Richmond Times Dispatch*: 'It was a serpent-like thing. It was swimming with its head out and then it started towards my boat. I've been a charter boat captain for 35 years and I've seen a lot of porpoises and turtles. This was different.'

In 1982 Chessie was videotaped by businessman Robert Frew, who with his wife and friends had a long sighting of it and estimated its length at about 30ft (9m). The video was blurred due to distance and heat, but it was convincing enough to be taken seriously by the Smithsonian Institute, whose conclusion was that it probably showed an animate object, although of indeterminate identity. Eels and oarfish were rejected on grounds of both appearance and behaviour. The 'giant snake from South America' theory was doubted by the scientists because an anaconda could probably not survive long in the conditions of Chesapeake Bay, and anyway would keep to the warm shallows and freshwater rivermouths.

Caddy

The opposite coast of North America likewise has sea serpents. The most famous, nicknamed 'Caddy' by journalists in the 1930s, is the so-called Cadborosaurus, Cadboro Bay in British Columbia being where it has been most commonly sighted; the local Native Americans call it Hiaschuckaluck. In fact the same beast has been spotted at various sites all along the British Columbia coast, though particularly in the 300-mile (500km) sound between Vancouver Island and the mainland.

Witnesses commonly describe it as having a camel- or horse-like head with large eyes, a long thin neck, a mane and a large body. Overall length is estimated variously at 40–70ft (12–20m). In 1946 sightings were so common that a plan was hatched to catch the serpent and put it on show in Vancouver's swimming pool; Caddy had enough friends for this idea to be scotched.

Many of the 1940s claims were ridiculed and many were undoubtedly hoaxes, but it is hard to disbelieve them all; such as the detailed testimony of Judge James Thomas Brown of the King's Bench of Saskatchewan who observed a 35–40 feet (11–12m) specimen while on holiday in 1950. And there have been continued sightings ever since.

There have also been reports of Caddy and Amy (the female of the species) mating. *The Vancouver Sun* for 30 October 1993 reported Dr Ed Bousfield, a retired associate of the Royal British Columbia Museum, as saying that two seaplane pilots had spotted a pair of sea monsters in Saanich Inlet, a common sighting place. The creatures were engaged in what appeared to be an intimate embrace and had the traditional 'loops' of the sea serpent. They swam away quickly when the plane landed in the bay.

On average there are at least half a dozen fresh sightings of Caddy per year. Bousfield accepts that a carcass or live specimen is needed before the creature's existence is established beyond doubt, but in April 1995 he went ahead anyway and with Paul LeBlond published an article in *Amphipacifica*, a quarterly biology journal. In it they dub the beast 'Cadborosaurus willsi', describing it as a large aquatic reptile. Their evidence consists mainly of eyewitness reports, but:

'in our view, the records do contain published evidence of "specimens in hand", and are sufficiently voluminous and internally consistent to conclude that the animal is real and merits formal taxonomic description'.

To back their case Bousfield and LeBlond had published a book, *Cadborosaurus: Survivor from the Deep* (1994).

Dr Bousfield is *the* Caddy expert and has collected over 200 accounts of Cadborosaurus sightings. His own theory is that Caddy is a surviving dinosaur, and he believes the females enter shallow estuaries to bear live young, as do garter snakes.

Under other names, the same or a similar creature is known further down the Pacific coast. California has the Old Man of Monterey, Bobo of Cape San Martin and the San Clemente Monster; all draw enthusiasts and have histories dating back as far as Caddy.

Sea Serpents Around the British Isles

Sea serpents have been seen all around Britain but especially along the fissured west coast of Scotland. There were many sightings in the early 19th century, including examples by clergymen and visitors that somehow carried more conviction with the general public than what sailors and islanders had been saying for centuries.

Morgawr, the Cornish sea monster

One of these witnesses was the Reverend Donald Maclean, who wrote to an inquiry in the Orkneys about a live monster he had encountered near the Hebridean island of Coll in June 1808. He was rowing with a friend along the coast when he noticed what he at first thought was a rock about half a mile (800m) distant. Knowing there should not be an islet there, he fixed his eye on it and to his alarm saw a small head rise out of the water on a long neck.

The two men headed rapidly for shore, watched for a while by the beast. Then it dived violently and gave chase. The terrified oarsmen paddled for their lives, scrambled ashore and climbed the nearest bank, then turned to see it:

'coming rapidly underwater towards the stern of our boat. When within a few yards of the boat, finding the water shallow, it raised its monstrous head above water and by a winding course got, with apparent difficulty, clear of the creek where our boat lay, and where the monster seemed in danger of being imbayed. It continued to move off, with its head above water, and with the wind, for about half a mile [800m] before we lost sight of it.

'Its head was rather broad, of a form somewhat oval. Its neck somewhat smaller. Its shoulders, if I can so term them, considerably broader, and thence it tapered towards the tail, which it kept pretty low in the water, so that a view of it could not be taken so distinctly as I wished. It had no fin that I could perceive, and seemed to me to move progressively by undulation up and down. Its length I believed to be from 70 to 80 feet [23m]'... About the time I saw it, it was seen about the Isle of Canna. The crews of thirteen fishing boats, I am told, were so much terrified at its appearance, that they in a body fled to the nearest creek.'

Half a century later a sea serpent returned to the Hebrides. In August 1872 it was seen by many witnesses, including two more clergymen, the Reverend John Macrae of Glenelg, Inverness-shire, and the Reverend David Twopenny of Stockbury, Kent. They were out boating in clear weather with family and friends in the channel between Skye and the mainland when they saw a dark mass 200yd (180m) behind them to the north. Through binoculars they observed a second lump rise to the left of the first, followed by several others. These humps began to move in such a way that they seemed part of a single creature – which disappeared, then resurfaced. The trippers had no clear view of the head, but what they took to be the head seemed always to surface first, followed by the humps. They estimated the overall length of the visible portion to be about 45ft (14m).

'Presently, as we were watching the creature, it began to approach us rapidly, causing a great agitation in the sea. Nearly the whole of the body had now disappeared, and the head advanced at a great rate in the midst of a shower of fine spray, which was evidently raised in some way by the quick movement of the animal and not by spouting. Miss Forbes was alarmed and retreated to the cabin, crying out that the creature was coming down upon us. When within about a hundred yards [90m] of us it sank and moved away in the direction of Skye just under the surface of the water, for we could trace its course by the waves it raised on the still sea to the distance of a mile or more. After that it continued at intervals to show itself, careering about at a distance as long as we were in that part of the Sound.'

Rather astonishingly, the party went boating again the next day in the same area, minus the sensible Miss Forbes. And again they saw the monster. This time it seemed even longer than before, lying more stretched-out on the surface, and they estimated its length as more like 60ft (18m). The story was widely published at the time, and many other witnesses came forward.

In Cornwall there is a sea monster of some kind called Morgawr – which simply means 'sea giant'. There have been sightings and reported strandings since forever, but there was particular excitement in the 1970s, when the *Falmouth Packet* and *Cornish Life* published many articles and even a few smudgy photographs. The creature was repeatedly described as 'looking like pictures of the Loch Ness Monster'. About 40ft (12m) long and greeny-grey in colour, it was sometimes seen accompanied by what was assumed to be its baby.

The indistinct photographs were reportedly taken in Falmouth Bay in February 1976 by a coy witness who identified herself only as Mary F. The *Falmouth Packet* published them in March along with her description of the creature looking like:

'an elephant waving its trunk, but the trunk was a long neck with a small head on the end, like a snake's head. It had humps on the back which moved in a funny way. The colour was black or very dark brown, and the skin seemed to be like a sea lion's ... the animal frightened me. I would not like to see it any closer. I do not like the way it moved when swimming.'

Far Eastern Sea Serpents

The sea serpent is as common in oriental folklore as in its occidental counterparts. In China the legends merge into purely mythical accounts of sea dragons, which have the disconcerting talent of shapeshifting, but the more credible tales seem to describe something very similar to the sea serpent, in China called the Kiao or Shan.

The Shan

The less fanciful accounts of the Kiao describe it as a cross between a dragon and a serpent, with a small head, fine neck and a girth of about 15ft (4.6m). A lake-dweller, it is said to be solitary. A possible distinction between it and the Shan is that the latter lives at sea. The Shan is described as serpentine but with ears, horns and a red mane. Until recently the Malays and Chinese believed sea serpents were responsible for ambergris, which they call 'dragon spittle'. In the *History of the Ming Dynasty*, a Chinese author describes a place called Dragon Spittle Island in the Sea of Lambri.

'Every spring, numerous Shan come together to play on this island and they leave behind their spittle. The natives afterwards go in canoes to the spot and collect this spittle ... When burnt it has a pure and delicious fragrance.'

It was sold in markets for over a hundred gold pieces per pound. Confusion comes from a common assertion that the Kiao Shan's breath looks like a column or tower, which must refer to whales spouting. But there are tales enough of monsters which cannot be whales.

The mouth of the Chien Tang river was once terrorized by a large sea serpent, as were many other estuaries. In some places virgins were sacrificed to appease the monster until some hero came along to slay the beast.

In the 19th century many oriental sea serpents were seen by Europeans. Some were shown to be frauds or hysterical exaggerations, but several accounts cannot be easily dismissed – though, as always, many witnesses regretted having gone public. The *Straits Times Overland Journal* carried a lively correspondence on the matter. Particularly dramatic was the encounter in September 1876 between the SS *Nestor* and a 'sea serpent' in the Straits of Malacca which seemed rather different to most, though very Chinese.

The creature first appeared about 200yd (180m) to starboard. About 200ft (60m) long, it kept pace with the steamer for a while before diving and resurfacing on the vessel's other side. All in all the beast was visible to passengers and crew for about half an hour. Many of these people came forward later with their individual versions of events, which were in broad agreement with that supplied by Captain John Webster:

'It had a square head and a dragon black and white striped tail, and an immense body, which was quite fifty feet [15m] broad when the monster raised it. The head was about twelve feet [3.7m] broad, and appeared to be, at the extreme, about six feet [1.8m] above the water ... The long dragon tail with black and white scales afterwards rose in an undulating motion, in which at one time the head, at another the body, and eventually the tail, formed each in its turn a prominent object above the water.'

One suggestion taken quite seriously at the time was that the 'Nestor' monster was not a serpent but a giant turtle. There is a healthy tradition in the Far East of giant marine turtles. Rather confusingly, they are often called 'shan' in China to distinguish them from common turtles, so some tales about Shan may refer either to sea serpents or giant turtles.

An ancient Book of Physiognomy appears to say that the name Kiao Shan means 'crossed eyebrows' but possibly something got lost in the translation. In both China and Japan the Kiao is said to sprout wings and take to the air when it reaches a certain age or size, emitting a beautiful music that sounds like 'singing stones'.

There is in the Far East a well-known living 'dragon' species, named the Komodo Dragon because its primary (almost its only) habitat is Indonesia's Komodo Island. This giant monitor lizard usually grows to about 12ft (3.7m), but specimens twice as long have been reported. The creatures migrate by sea between Komodo and three other Indonesian islands. Specimens washed out to sea may well have given rise to some sea-monster tales, but none of great importance.

OPPOSITE:

The Chien Tang

river monster

3
OTHER MONSTERS OF THE DEEP

A giant squid

But serpents are not the only monsters in the sea. By a happy coincidence, while Eggleton was in Australia during the course of completing the last few paintings for this book a 'hairy blob' was washed up on the shore of Tasmania, stirring local memories of the legendary 'Water Yowie' that was washed ashore there in 1960. The earlier enigma lay on the beach for nearly two years before suddenly achieving world fame and totally stumping naturalists as to what it might be. DNA testing on the 1997 'globster' seemed to show that it was simply a mass of whale blubber. Which is disappointing, as it suggests that the 1960 one was the same. However, there are other monsters aplenty in the deep …

Giant Squid

Giant squid are true sea monsters, as alien and terrifying as anything born from one's nightmares. A surprising number of people still believe them a myth sprung from Jules Verne's 20,000 Leagues Under the Sea *(1870), but since the 19th century their existence has been officially recognized.*

How many species there are in the genus *Architeuthis* remains a mystery, because the proportions of the specimens so far recovered vary wildly. For a while almost every large squid found was allotted a new *Architeuthis* species, but naturalists have since calmed down and are waiting for the situation to clarify itself.

Like all squid, the giants are carnivorous cephalopods related to the octopus and cuttlefish. But, while the octopus likes to lurk in caves and the cuttlefish lies disguised on the seabed, snatching passing prey with its extending jaws, the squid is a free-roaming inhabitant of the deep. It propels itself in a motion rather like a manta ray's, using lobe-shaped caudal fins at the end of its body. It can also jet-propel itself in any direction by squirting water from a movable siphon at the base of its head. In emergencies the same jet squirts out a cloud of ink as a cover for escape. Unlike most squid, the giant is believed to be rather solitary in its habits. Its physique suggests it is also rather lethargic, although it is capable of astonishing bursts of speed.

The long torpedo-shaped body, or mantle, is soft and fleshy and supported by an internal skeleton, as with the cuttlefish. If non-giant squid can be taken as a guide, both the colour and the texture of the skin can change rapidly according to the creature's mood or need to camouflage itself.

Below the body are two enormous eyes, the largest in the animal kingdom. Vision seems important to all squid. The giant squid's eyes can be up to 18in (46cm) across and look unnervingly like human eyes, with a pupil, iris and cornea. These eyes are, in fact, the closest in design of any invertebrate's to our own – right down to the retinas having rods and cones – but the similarity has occurred through parallel evolution rather than any genetic relationship. Rapidly changing colour displays are an intricate part of the squid's body language, and many can produce subtle and dramatic luminous patterns on their skin.

Below the eyes is a beak-shaped mouth powerful enough to cut steel cables. This is surrounded by eight arms, each with a double row of stalk-mounted suckers ringed with sharp 'teeth'. If it loses these arms in battle the squid is able to regrow them. Like cuttlefish, squid also have a pair of tentacles, often twice as long as the arms and ending in a paddle or hook, which the creature uses to grasp prey and drag it into the mouth.

Giant squid feed on fish, dolphins, porpoises and even whales. Anything live that comes their way, in fact, including humans. Apart from whales they have no real predators, but while growing they are vulnerable to any marine carnivore larger than themselves. They leap this hurdle by growing very rapidly.

The squid was well known in the Mediterranean in ancient times. Aristotle, Pliny and many others described it.

Aristotle said there was a common squid, *teuthis*, which was only about a foot (30cm) long and a larger, rarer variety, *teuthos*, which grew up to eight or nine feet (2.5m). He hinted at the possibility of still larger varieties inhabiting the open seas, but made no guess as to their size. Of their appearance he said these giants were rumoured to be 'like shields, red in colour and with many fins'.

For over 1,000 years the scientific consensus in Europe agreed more or less with Aristotle. There must have been sightings of giant squid, stranded or out in the open sea, but they remained rumours which few took seriously. The significant next mention of what is probably a giant squid was by Olaus Magnus (1490–1557) in his *Historia de Gentibus Septentrionalibus* (1555); he speaks of giant fish whose 'Forms are horrible, their Heads square, all set with prickles, and they have sharp and long Horns around about, like a Tree rooted up by the Roots'. The heads were supposed to be up to 24ft (7m) long, black, and with huge eyes which glowed like fire beneath the waves at night. The main tentacles were about 30ft (9m) long. Magnus heard rumours that 'One of these Sea-Monsters will drown easily many great ships provided with many strong Mariners'.

Olaus Magnus, like Pontoppidan, was widely dismissed as a fantasist, but time would prove he was not exaggerating. In 1673 a giant squid was washed up on southwest Ireland's Dingle Peninsula, It was not quite the size of Olaus Magnus's 'monstrous fish', but close enough. It became famous through a travelling show that displayed bits of the carcass, including two arms and the pharynx, which, like that of the creature in the *Alien* movies, is a beaked mouth capable of shooting out a yard (90cm) or so to grab prey. Its 'head' was described as having 'two great eyes, and the creature was measured at about 19ft (6m) in length, 'bigger in the body than any horse'. The arms, also described as 'horns', were about 8ft (2.5m) long and the tentacles extended at least 11ft (3.4m), though they were probably broken off short by the time the measurements were being made. 'Over this monster's back was a mantle of bright red colour, with a fringe round it, it hung down on both sides like a carpet on a table, falling back on each side.'

Reports of even larger squid came in during the following century or so, but were largely dismissed by naturalists. During the 19th century, however, the evidence grew to the point that in about 1850 the giant squid was finally given the taxonomic name *Architeuthis monachus* by the Danish zoologist Johan Japetus Steenstrup (1813–1897).

Some were still not convinced, but in November 1861 the French gunboat *Alecton* came upon a giant squid struggling on the surface near Tenerife. The crew tried to haul it aboard but the creature broke up under its own weight. Its length from tail-tip to mouth was estimated at about 18ft (5.5m). Still not everyone was convinced, but in the 1870s a glut of giant squid washed ashore along the foundland coast put an end to scepticism. Some of the beasts even attacked fishermen, who saved

Look out from below

themselves by cutting off the arms. The cause of this glut was probably a shift in the counter-flowing cold Labrador current and the warm Gulf Stream. Squid appear to be very temperature-sensitive, and when the water is too warm they lose control of both their buoyancy and the oxygen flow in their blood. So most giant-squid sightings are of creatures in trouble in similar areas of mixed current.

The largest of the Newfoundland strandings was at Thimble Tickle on 2 November 1878. The squid was partially beached and trying to struggle back to the sea when three fishermen spotted it. Thinking it was a wreck, they rowed over and, as reported in the *Boston Traveller*:

'to their horror, found themselves close to a huge fish, having large glassy eyes, which was making desperate efforts to escape, and churning the water into foam by the motion of its immense arms and tail. It was aground and the tide was ebbing. From the funnel at the back of its head it was ejecting large volumes of water, this being its method of moving backwards.'

The fishermen hooked it with an anchor on a stout rope, which they then tied to a tree; the unfortunate squid therefore died when the tide went out. Before chopping the carcass up for dog-food they measured it at 20ft (6m) from beak to tail. The longest tentacles attained 35ft (11m) and the legs were about the same length as the body, with suckers up to 4in (10cm) across. So, finally, Olaus Magnus was proved not to have been overstating the case.

The Thimble Tickle squid is generally rated the largest yet found, but there are fairly reliable reports of much bigger ones. A case in point is the specimen discovered in 1892 trapped beneath a log raft on the west coast of Canada, near Port Simpson. Its long tentacles were estimated to be over 100ft (30m) in length and its largest suckers were said to be as big as dinner plates.

As the true dimensions of giant squid were becoming apparent, whalers told tales of the bizarre oceanic feud between these beasts and sperm whales. When sperm whales are fighting for their lives they vomit up the contents of their stomach. This usually consists mainly of squid — in small, large and occasionally gigantic pieces. Tentacles up to 40ft (12m) long have been found, with suckers 'as big as a dinner plate'. This conjures horrific images of how the squid met their end, but people have actually witnessed the battle.

A slightly fictionalized account is given by Frank Bullen in his *The Cruise of the Cachalot* (1898), based on his experience as a young deckhand on a whaler. In 1875 he was on watch one bright moonlit night in the Straits of Malacca when he saw a commotion out to sea. Night glasses revealed that:

'a very large sperm whale was locked in deadly conflict with a cuttle-fish, or squid, almost as large as himself, whose interminable tentacles seemed to enlace the whole of his great body. The head of the whale especially seemed a perfect network of writhing arms — naturally, I suppose, for it appeared as if the whale had the tail part of the mollusc in his jaws, and, in a businesslike, methodical way, was sawing through it. By the side of the black columnar head of the whale appeared the head of the great squid, as awful an object as one could well imagine in a fevered dream. Judging as carefully as possible, I estimated it to be at least as large as one of our pipes [barrels], which contained three hundred and fifty gallons; but it may have been, and probably was, a good deal larger. The eyes were remarkable from their size and blackness, which, contrasted with the livid whiteness of the head, made their appearance all the more striking. They were at least a foot in diameter and, seen under such conditions, looked decidedly eerie and hobgoblin-like.

All around the combatants were numerous sharks, like jackals round a lion, ready to share the feast, and apparently assisting in the destruction of the huge cephalopod.'

Whalers once believed that the squid always came off worst in such contests, but this is not necessarily so. In 1965 the crew of the Soviet whaler *Mirny* witnessed a battle between a giant squid and a 40-ton sperm whale which neither survived: the whale was strangled, but not before it had succeeded in biting the squid's head off. And in October 1966 two lighthouse-keepers at Danger Point near Cape Town witnessed a baby southern right whale being attacked by a giant squid. For an hour and a half the monster clung to the infant, apparently trying to drown it, while the mother whale looked on helplessly. Finally the struggling pair went under, never to reappear.

Such titanic battles helped explain something which had long puzzled whalers – circular scars on whaleskin. It became clear that these scars were inflicted by the toothed 'suckers' of giant squid. They are so common that there is clearly a running war between giant squid and whales.

Squid soon dissolve in a whale's stomach except for their beaks. Some sperm whales have been found with several thousand beaks in their stomach. Taking this and an estimate of the number of whales in the sea, it has been reasonably suggested that squid may be the commonest creatures on the planet. One calculation has even suggested that the amount of squid consumed in any one year by whales and other marine predators could exceed the combined bodymass of the human species; this seems unlikely but is not impossible, because squid seem to be the favourite food of almost anything larger than themselves in the sea, including other squid. They survive the carnage by having a phenomenal rate of reproduction. Giant squid form only a tiny percentage of the total, obviously, but even so their true number is probably still large enough to boggle the mind.

The circular scars on whales also show that the Thimble Tickle giant squid was no great exception in size – in fact, it seems monsters twice as big are probably common. What we should make of scars 18in (46cm) across is something no one has been brave enough to suggest. They could be scars suffered long ago that have expanded as the whale has grown, or they could have a totally different cause. But they may also be telling us that, when it comes to giant squid, we ain't seen nothing yet.

Someone who would agree is A.G. Starkey, who was on a British Admiralty trawler near the Maldive Islands during the Second World War. One night as he was fishing over the side, alone on deck and using a cluster of lightbulbs to attract fish, he had the unnerving experience of attracting something else entirely. Rising out of the depths towards him came an enormous, green, unwinking eye surrounded by a strange commotion of the water. Gradually and to his horror he realized he was staring almost

Battle of the sperm whale and giant squid.

point-blank at a vast squid. 'I am not squeamish, but that cold, malevolent, unblinking eye seemed to be looking directly at me. I don't think I have ever seen anything so coldly hypnotic and intelligent before or since.' Taking a torch, he walked up and down the length of the ship examining the creature lying alongside. 'The ship was about 175ft (53m) in length ... but the squid was longer. It remained alongside for about a quarter of an hour before zooming effortlessly away into the night.

The impression of intelligence given by a squid's eyes, as mentioned by Starkey and many others, is largely due to their similarity to our own, but it is perhaps worth mentioning that squid and other cephalopods are the only invertebrates to possess recognizable brains. Squid themselves are not very amenable to laboratory tests, but the sedentary octopus has shown signs of remarkable intelligence and ingenuity.

A curious incident in the 1930s proves that squid can sometimes be reckless aggressors and may well attack whales larger than themselves. The Royal Norwegian Navy vessel *Brunswick*, a 15,000-ton auxiliary tanker, was cruising the Pacific between Hawaii and Samoa at about 12 knots (22kph) when it was overtaken from behind by a 30ft (9m) squid. This swam alongside for a bit, then swung in and rammed the 500ft (150m) ship in the side. Unable to get a grip on the steel hull, the squid then slithered to the stern and was turned to mincemeat by the propellers.

This was startling enough, but it then happened twice again soon after, for reasons that remain a mystery. If the ship had been smaller and the squid real giants, the encounter could have turned into a sailor's worst nightmare.

Vampyre Squid

Giant squid are not the only ones to fear. In 1991 a cameraman, Alex Kerstitch, was attacked by some human-sized squid he was filming off the coast of California. Three of them grabbed him and tried to drag him down into the depths, strangling him all the while. Then, luckily, they changed their minds for no apparent reason.

Kerstitch wrote later that he now totally understood Victor Hugo's description of the squid's cousin, the octopus, as a 'nightmarish sea-vampire'. He said his experience felt exactly as horrible as one would imagine.

Humans only rarely meet large squid by chance – you generally have to go looking for them. Luckily, you are even less likely to run into the 'vampyre squid of the infernal deep', *Vampyroteuthis infernalis*. It is found in all the oceans, but lives at depths of 3,000ft (900m) or more.

The vampyre squid is a horrible little creature, less than a foot (30cm) long, with eight short, webbed legs and two tentacles which it keeps tucked away in sacs. It is deep black in colour, but has gleaming white jaws and bright red eyes over an inch (2.5cm) in diameter. It is very weakly muscled, and appears to subsist by hovering in the deep and stealthily attaching itself to passing prey and sucking their juices.

Merhorses

Many witnesses of sea serpents describe them as having a maned head rather like a horse's, but there are also creatures specifically called merhorses. There must be some overlap between the two types of sighting – perhaps the distinction is simply related to size, with the larger creatures being called serpents and the smaller ones merhorses.

Accounts of merhorses tail off into the purely fantastical realm of beautiful mermaids, for in the Middle Ages it was popularly believed that every creature on land had its marine counterpart – at the extreme this even included mer-bishops, complete with mitres on their heads! But there seems enough evidence to suggest that the merhorse may possibly be a distinct and genuine species.

The creature is described as having a long reddish mane and a slender, medium-length neck. Only one hump shows on the surface. The merhorse's very large eyes look forward, suggesting it is a predator, and the beast has long hairs or whiskers on its face. The head has also been described as resembling a camel's from the side, but as being so wide that from the front it looks almost like a snake's. The wet skin appears shiny, as if covered in fur, and is either a uniform dark brown or black. Sometimes a ragged crest down the back has been reported. The merhorse undulates vertically when swimming, like the seal – to which some believe it is related. Reported lengths are usually up to about 30ft (9m), but are sometimes more – and this is where confusion with the sea serpent creeps in.

Merhorse

Sightings of merhorses are not very common, but they come from all over the world, mostly from temperate zones and fairly near the coast. One credible sighting was by A.G. Thompson, as described in his *Gower Journey* 1950). He was looking down from the cliffs onto Fall Bay situated on the Gower Peninsula in southwest Wales – and saw what at first he took for a log about 30ft (9m) long. Then it raised from the water a maned head like that of a horse. It watched something on the shore for a while before diving from view with a curious double undulation. Thompson watched for a further half-hour but there was no reappearance. A local expert was of the opinion that it was a 'real sea-horse'.

Red Herrings

*Even ignoring hoaxes, lies and exaggerations, many sightings of
sea monsters can still be easily explained in terms of the known.
A log snagged to the sea bed can seem to swim against the tide,
mats of seaweed may surface briefly, and mirages caused by
thermal inversions are common near water surfaces and can
create a lens effect that completely distorts scale, perspective
and even outline.*

A known kind of monster can be mistaken for an unknown one – we saw this as a possible explanation of the Egede sighting (see page 8). It has been plausibly suggested that the 'Daedalus incident' (see page 9) might also be explained as involving a giant squid imperfectly seen on the surface.

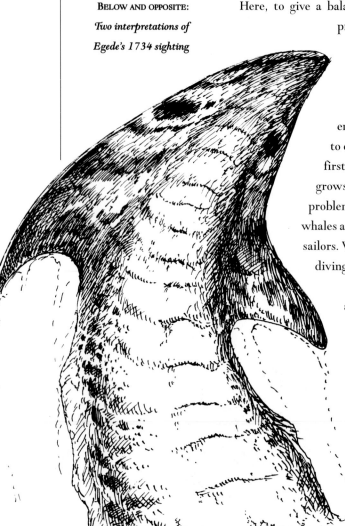

BELOW AND OPPOSITE:

*Two interpretations of
Egede's 1734 sighting*

Here, to give a balanced picture, we survey a few of the distractions that have probably done the cause of cryptozoology more harm than good, as they tend to be used as ammunition against the case for the existence of unknown sea monsters.

Whales and sharks could in some circumstances be mistaken for unknown monsters, and certainly they are big enough. The largest whale, the blue whale, can comfortably grow to over 100ft (30m) in length. The largest shark is the whale shark, first discovered in 1828 off the tip of South Africa; it commonly grows to 40ft (12m) in length but can reach over 60ft (18m). The problem with any rationalization involving these creatures is that both whales and sharks are easily recognizable from a distance, particularly by sailors. Whales spout and give a characteristic flourish of the tail when diving, and sharks have that famously prominent dorsal fin.

The basking shark is another matter. It grows up to 40ft (12m), and it would not be surprising if some grew half as long again. When alive the basking shark is as obvious as any other kind of shark, but when dead it presents a very different picture, and dead specimens have probably caused more excitement about 'sea serpents' than any of the species' cousins.

Down the centuries there have been many reports of carcasses being washed ashore that look remarkably like that of a plesiosaur – small head, long thin neck, bulbous body and lozenge-shaped swimming fins. The most famous 19th-century example was the Stronsay Beast, washed ashore in the Orkney Islands in the autumn of 1808. Several locals went to investigate and agreed it was 55ft (17m) long, appeared to have a head no larger than a seal's, a long neck, a bulbous body, a frilly dorsal fin and a winding, pointed tail. Thanks to the interest of local dignitaries, this discovery soon became national news – and, as there had already been rumours (see page 56) of sea serpents among the Hebridean islands, likewise off northern Scotland, people naturally assumed one of these had died. The Stronsay carcass became a sensation. Even before he had seen all the evidence, Patrick Neill, Secretary of the Wernerian Natural History Society in Edinburgh, pronounced that 'no doubt could be entertained that this was the kind of animal described by Ramus, Egede and Pontoppidan, but which scientific and systematic naturalists had hitherto rejected as spurious and ideal'.

When evidence did arrive, in the form of affidavits from witnesses and detailed diagrams of the cranium, sternum and several vertebrae, the creature was solemnly christened *Halsydrus Pontoppidani*, or Pontoppidan's Sea Serpent. Sadly this taxonomic conceit fell apart when the same evidence was presented to Sir Everard Home, first President of the Royal College of Surgeons in London, who had a side interest in sea monsters. He immediately recognized the samples as identical to some in his possession that were known to come from basking sharks. And, once he made this identification, it suddenly seemed obvious to other naturalists.

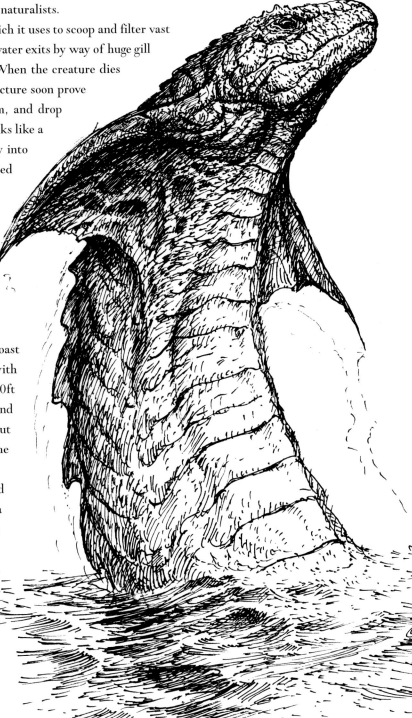

The basking shark has an enormous mouth, which it uses to scoop and filter vast quantities of water for plankton and shrimp. The water exits by way of huge gill slits which almost completely encircle the head. When the creature dies and begins to decompose the jawbone and gill structure soon prove too heavy for the slender tissues supporting them, and drop away to leave a tiny cranium at the end of what looks like a thin neck. The dorsal fin, too, decomposes quickly into hair-like strands; this explains the 'dorsal crest' noted by observers of the Stronsay carcass. The lower lobe of the tail fluke drops away so that it looks as though the living creature had a tail that tapered to a single point. Hey Presto! A dead basking shark takes on the outline of a plesiosaur, one of the favourite candidates for the sea serpent.

In 1934 a similar creature was washed ashore at Querqueville on the French coast facing England. Some fishermen found a carcass with a small head, a slender neck 3ft (90cm) long and a 30ft (9m) body with two large flippers near the front and a tapering tail. This caused great excitement, but again professional examination revealed it to be the remains of a basking shark.

In April 1977 the whole story was repeated when the Japanese trawler *Zuiyo Maru* dragged a strange carcass from the deep near New Zealand; the fishermen managed to photograph it before the stench became too much and they dumped the corpse back into the sea. The picture was flashed around the world and scientists at Yokohama University and elsewhere came to the conclusion that the trawler had netted a recently deceased plesiosaur. However, samples of tissue analyzed at Tokyo University were found to contain elastodin, a protein found only in sharks and rays. So almost certainly this was just another rotting basking shark.

Obviously, however disappointing such cases might be to those who would like to prove the continuing existence of plesiosaurs, they do not actually disprove the theory. For example, although there proved to be a perfectly mundane explanation for the Stronsay Beast, we still have no positive identification for the live sea monster that chased the Reverend Donald Maclean in the Hebrides a few months earlier (see page 56). Curiously, the Querqueville carcass also showed up soon after sailors reported having seen a live sea

The Zuiyo Maru catch

serpent, this time in the English Channel, and this happenstance was one reason why everyone leapt to the conclusions they did.

Eels have been mentioned as a possible explanation of sea serpents but, as we have seen, their sideways undulation when swimming means they could possibly account for at best a few sightings. Nevertheless, eels may possibly grow to monstrous size. In February 1930 the Danish oceanologist Anton Bruun, collecting marine samples from the ship *Dana* in the South Atlantic near the Cape of Good Hope, caught what appeared to be an eel larva 6ft (1.8m) long. The specimen, hauled up from 150 fathoms (270m), had 450 vertebrae, three times as many as in the largest classified eel.

Calculating according to the average relative proportions of larva and adult in common eels, this giant specimen suggested an adult marine eel 60–70ft (18–21m) long – oversimplified calculation, of course, because there is no guarantee that those relative proportions are the same from species to species. There have been suggestions that the specimen was not an eel larva at all, but Bruun himself was convinced enough to stick by his original identification. If nothing else, he said, the discovery prompted the question that, if this backboned creature could survive unknown at such depths, why could not the sea serpent?

The Sargasso Sea was once believed to be the breeding ground of sea monsters and was superstitiously avoided by early transatlantic sailors. This strange area, a slow-moving whirlpool several hundred miles across with a floating carpet of *Sargassum* weed, has since proved no threat at all to shipping: the blanket of weed is nowhere near thick enough to entangle a ship and sightings of sea monsters are, if anything, less likely here than in many other regions, such as the North Atlantic. Nevertheless the area has a curious link to one kind of 'sea serpent'. Study of the Sargasso Sea has solved a long-standing riddle: where do freshwater eels go to mate? The answer is that all freshwater eels, whether from Europe or from North America, swim to the Sargasso Sea, then make the long journey back to their home river. For British eels this excursion can take two to three years.

The oarfish is another marine creature responsible for a few sea-serpent reports. Known also as the 'King of the Herrings', because it was once believed to lead herring shoals, the oarfish is a long eel-like creature with a flat, silvery body. It is so thin that it is sometimes called the ribbonfish, and so fragile that it is no danger to anything apart from smaller fish. Down the length of its back it has a spiky, crimson dorsal fin. It commonly grows to 25ft (7.5m) long but examples have been reported at twice that length. It lives deep down, so is only rarely stranded or caught. It has a worldwide spread.

It is tempting to rechristen the oarfish the 'King of Red Herrings', but sadly the creature has not really influenced the debate about sea serpents to any great extent. The obvious bright red mane and silvery body are rarely mentioned in sea-serpent accounts. Moreover, the oarfish is unable to raise its head above the waves for any length of time. When washed ashore, an accident which has occured in Bermuda, the creatures can startle people who come across them suddenly, but they are too weak on land to make any aggressive movements.

Although it is no longer a very popular theory, it has been suggested that sea serpents may be mammals – giant long-necked seals, in fact. This is not quite as unlikely as it sounds. The elephant seal can grow to almost 30ft (9m) in length and can weigh up to three tons.

There is also the matter of Steller's sea cow, a large mammal discovered in the Bering Straits during the 18th century and quickly hunted to probable extinction; this relative of the dugong, grew to a length of 40ft (12m) and in certain conditions might well assume the profile of a plesiosaur, albeit with a slightly short neck. If Steller's sea cow escaped being wiped out – and there have been possible recent sightings in the northern Pacific – it could account for some sea-serpent sightings in that area. Should it have cousins in other oceans, again these might be responsible for some sea-serpent and merhorse sightings. Support for this notion is dwindling, however, partly because other mammals of this group – including the dugong and the manatee – cannot give birth at sea but instead must do so on land or ice.

OPPOSITE:

Sargasso Sea

Living Dinosaurs

The most popular and plausible explanation for sea serpents
and lake monsters is that they are species of surviving dinosaur.
Many possible candidates have been suggested, particularly
when allowance is made for several million years of possible
further evolution since the time of fossil specimens, but a few
names crop up repeatedly.

Pleisiosaurs

PLESIOSAUR. These creatures were first described amid great excitement in 1823. Baron Georges Cuvier (1769–1832), the great naturalist and 'Father of Palaeontology', said:

'The *Plesiosaurus* is perhaps the strangest of the inhabitants of the ancient world and the one which seems most to deserve the name of monster.'

Whether one agrees with this is a matter of personal taste – most people would now give the title to something like *Tyrannosaurus rex*. But the plesiosaur is the most popular contender to explain sea-serpent and lake-monster sightings.

The plesiosaur was one of a group of sea-dwelling carnivorous reptiles that flourished about 200–65 million years ago, from the late Triassic period to the end of the Cretaceous period. It had a small snake-like head at the end of a long neck, a plump body with four strong, turtle-like flippers and a short tail. The subgroup known as pliosaurs had a larger head and a shorter neck, and commonly grew to a length of about 40ft (12m), which makes pliosaurs, and plesiosaurs in general, quite small for sea serpents, but if plesiosaurs

of any type have survived they may well have evolved into something slightly different, perhaps larger and with a longer tail and patterns of behaviour that, as with the giant squid, tend to keep it away from human observation.

THE ELASMOSAUR, one of the plesiosaur's immediate descendants, is an even better candidate for the sea serpent, but it hasn't caught on so well in the public imagination. It was larger and its even longer, thinner neck accounted for more than half its total length. *Mosasaur*

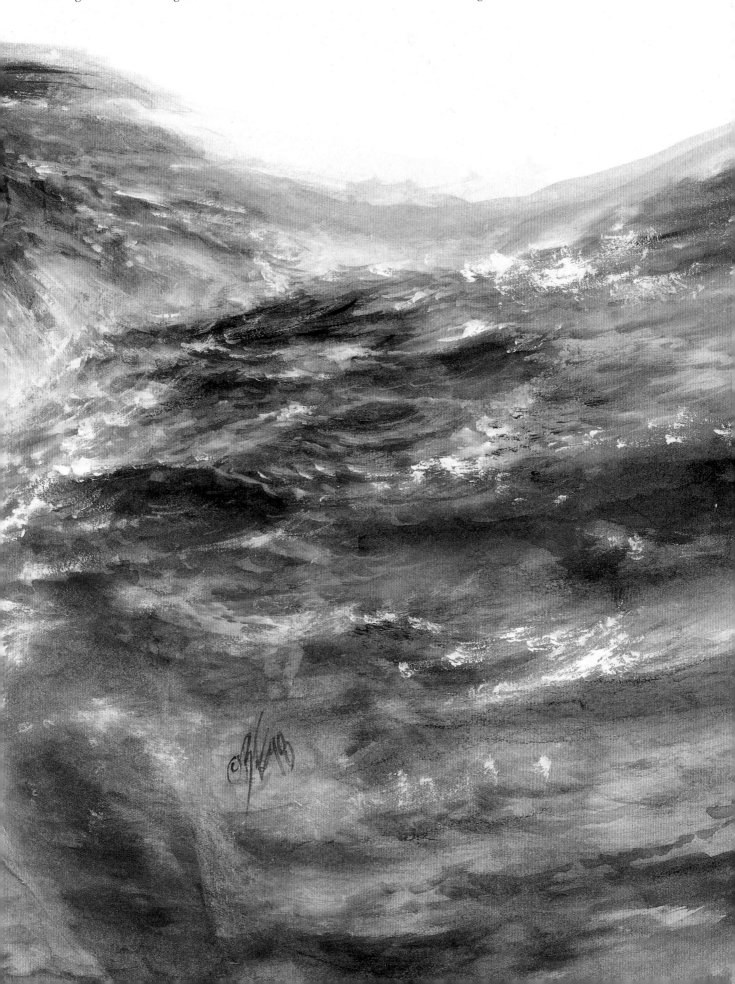

MOSASAUR. The first mosasaur fossil was discovered on the banks of the River Meuse near Maastricht in Holland in 1770; the name means 'Meuse dragon'. Similar in shape to modern lizards but much larger and with flippers for feet, mosasaurs had long jaws full of teeth and slightly resembled crocodiles. Like some snakes, they could deliberately dislocate their jaws to swallow large prey. It is likely they had a crest running the length of their back, and this might resemble a series of closely spaced humps if seen in suitable circumstances. Mosasaurs were closely related to several surviving species such as monitor lizards, Gila monsters and the Komodo dragon. Their skeleton appears to have been adapted to coping with enormous pressures but, being air-breathers, they would have had to return to the surface regularly, like whales.

The main argument against the mosasaur being the sea serpent is that it had a short neck, quite unlike the 'swan neck' described by so many witnesses of sea serpents and lake monsters.

THALATTOSUCHIA. These sea crocodiles had flippers for legs and a fish-tail at the rear. Several varieties existed during the last days of the dinosaurs. It has been suggested that some of the large crocodiles seen far out at sea may in fact be surviving thalattosuchians, particularly if they are observed to have their head and neck raised out of the water, as this is something true crocodiles cannot do for any length of time.

ZEUGLODON. Often suggested as a possible explanation for sea monsters, this was a marine mammal, the ancestor of modern whales. It had a long serpentine body, which at first seems a very promising attribute for the purposes of this argument, but unfortunately it also had a short neck, and this feature disqualifies it from responsibility for most sightings. The zeuglodon slightly resembled the mosasaur, but had only one pair of flippers near the front.

In 1845 'Doctor' Albert C. Koch exhibited on Broadway a 114ft (35m) skeleton of a 'fossil sea serpent' unearthed in Alabama. This created a sensation, but was quickly proved to be a fraud assembled from the remains of several different Alabaman zeuglodons. Accordingly, the show moved on rapidly; but several years later it was still touring Europe and making the same claims.

OPPOSITE:

Elasmosaur

Secret of the lake

4
LAKE MONSTERS

The beauty of lake monsters is that their domain is clearly defined. They are, as it were, like domestic sea serpents. Few of us will ever have the chance to check out the Atlantic or Pacific trenches for ourselves; but most of us can, if we're prepared to make the effort, experience at first hand the frisson of gazing out over a lake in the slight but tangible hope of seeing a monster pop its head above the waves. There are rumoured to be monsters in over 250 lakes, on all continents save the Antarctic. Features shared by most of these lakes are that they were connected with the sea during the last major glaciation and that they either are or were on the spawning routes of fish such as salmon.

*From the bottom of a
dark Scottish loch*

Half the fascination of lake monsters is that the dreaming part of our brain believes there should be monsters in lakes, just as there should be dragons or gods behind thunder. Science may have cleared the sky of dragons, but lakes and oceans retain the possibility of surprising us. Monsters of the deep preserve a spark of primaeval wonder ...

Nessie

The most famous lake monster of all is the Loch Ness Monster, largely because in the 1930s the world's press latched on to a spate of sightings at the loch. If the hand had been dealt differently, some other monster like Nahuelito (see page 90) might have grabbed the crown. But Nessie was the lucky one, and reigns supreme. The main cause of the original fuss is generally reckoned to be the decision to build a road along the north shore of the loch in 1933; this not only vastly increased the number of visitors to the area but, so believers say, must have stirred up the lake's creatures because of the blasting and the tipping of rocks into the water. No doubt the zeitgeist of the 1930s also played its part, but Nessie owes her fame primarily to a bureaucratic decision about traffic flow.

There had been rumours of a monster in Loch Ness long before. The earliest on record is the famous tale of St Columba's encounter with Nessie. St Columba of Iona (521–597) was, along with Patrick and Brigit, one of the three patron saints of Ireland, but at the age of 40 he got into a little political trouble at home, and as penance, was sent across the water to proselytize the Scots. From his base on the holy isle of Iona, which had long been a druid centre, he made forays across Scotland preaching Celtic Christianity.

St Adomnan's *Life of St Columba*, written by one of his successors about a century later, tells us (Book II, Chapter 28) that in the year 565 Columba was on his way to visit a local Pictish king, which journey required him to cross the River Ness. Close to the shore he met some people burying a friend who, they said, had been attacked and killed by the monster as he was swimming. They had only just succeeded in rescuing his body from the beast.

'The blessed man, on hearing this, was so far from being dismayed that he directed one of his companions to swim over and row across the ferry that was moored at the further bank. And Lugne Mocumin, hearing the command, obeyed without the least delay, taking off all his clothes except his tunic and leaping into the water. But the monster lying at the bottom of the stream, so far from being satiated, was only roused for more prey. When it felt the water disturbed above by the man swimming, it suddenly rushed out and, giving an awful roar, darted after him with its mouth wide open, as the man swam in the middle of the stream.

'Columba raised his holy hand while all the rest, brethren as well as strangers, were stupefied with terror. Invoking the name of God, he formed the saving sign of the cross in the air, and commanded the ferocious monster, saying, "Thou shalt go no further, nor touch the man; return with all speed."

'Then at the voice of the saint, the monster was terrified, and fled more quickly than if it had been pulled back with ropes, though it had got so near to Lugne, as he swam, that there was not more than the length of a spear-staff between the man and the beast.

'Then the brethren, seeing that the monster had gone back and that their comrade Lugne returned to them in the boat safe and sound, were struck with admiration, and gave glory to God in the blessed man. And even the barbarous heathens, who were present, were forced by the greatness of this miracle, which they themselves had seen, to magnify the God of the Christians.'

There then comes a long gap in the written records, though probably more because of their fragmentary nature than because Columba had frightened the monster into hiding for 1,000 years. In his *History of Scotland* (1527), Hector Boece (c1465–1536) records how early one midsummer morning the beast crawled out of the waters, overturning trees in its path, and killed three of the men who chased it. Their companions took to the trees and after a while the beast returned to the loch without harming them. It was from one of the survivors, Donald Campbell, that Boece claimed to have had the tale. Thereafter there are occasional mentions of the beast and certainly there was a local tradition of its existence, but the loch was extremely remote from the rest of the world until the 1930s.

Among the early newspaper stories that kindled the Nessie craze was one told by a water bailiff, Alex Campbell, who like his father before him was in charge of salmon stocks in Loch Ness. His tale, one of dozens of similar ones in circulation at the time, is among the most graphic and convincing. According to the *Inverness Courier*, early on the morning of 8 May 1933 Campbell was standing on the shore of Loch Ness where the Oich River enters it. The day was clear and calm, and Campbell was scanning the sky to see if any weather change was on the way. Suddenly the head and shoulders of a strange beast rose out of the water a dozen or so paces from the shore. The head, on a slender neck the height of a man, looked like that of a lizard. Beyond it, breaking the surface of the lake, appeared a hump which Campbell took to be the beast's body; he estimated it was about 30ft (9m) long. After a brief interval, during which the creature looked from side to side, Nessie sank into the waters and disappeared.

When he got home Campbell consulted an encyclopedia. The creature which most closely matched what he had seen was the supposedly long-extinct plesiosaur – this fossil reptile has remained one of the most popular contenders for Nessie's identity. This article was the first to give the creature the name it has borne since: the Loch Ness Monster. Campbell himself saw the beast over a dozen more times before his death in the late 1970s.

In October 1933 the *Inverness Courier* told the tale of William MacGruer, who had lived all his life in Fort Augustus. He said that over 20 years before he had been among a party of several children aged between 10 and 12 hunting for birds around Inchnacardoch Bay. Not far from the road they saw a strange creature emerge from some bushes and make for the loch, only a few yards away, where it dived into the water and disappeared. MacGruer said the beast reminded them of nothing so much as a miniature camel: it had a long neck, a humped back and 'fairly long legs'.

MacGruer's recollection was prompted by other accounts in the *Inverness Courier* of a monster being sighted on the new road. In the early morning of 22 July 1933 Mr and Mrs G. Spicer were on their way home from holiday in northern Scotland. Driving beside Loch Ness between Dores and Inverfarigaig, they met 'a most extraordinary form of animal' crossing the road ahead, making for the loch. They first saw a long thin neck, undulating with several arches, then a huge body which lumbered across the road and

OPPOSITE:

St Colombia and the

Loch Ness Monster

down to the water. The Spicers stopped when they reached the spot but could see nothing more than a large gap in the undergrowth where the creature must have passed.

Even scarier was the experience of Arthur Grant in January the following year. He almost ran into a similar beast on his motorbike while driving home from Inverness at half past one in the morning. It was a bright moonlit night, which was probably just as well because he might otherwise not have noticed the large creature lurking on the right of the road. It turned to stare at him, then lurched across the road, crashed through the undergrowth and dived into the loch with a loud splash.

Grant stopped and gave chase but there was nothing to see. He described the beast as being 15–20ft (4.5–6m) long with a small, snake-like head held about man-height on a long thin neck. The rounded body had massive hindquarters and a thick tail about 6ft (1.8m) long. The creature appeared to have two sets of flippers and its mode of propulsion on land was like that of a seal or sea-lion.

Such tales attracted hordes of photographers and sightseers to Loch Ness. The first plausible photo of Nessie was taken on 12 November 1933 by Hugh Gray, a worker for British Aluminium. He said he had taken a Sunday stroll along the lochside half a mile (800m) below Foyers, armed with a camera. While looking down on the lake from a height of about 30ft (9m) he noticed a commotion and saw a large body rise to the surface, stretching out a long thin neck. He managed to take five snaps before it sank from view again. Four of his exposures turned out blank when the film was processed three weeks later, but the fifth blurrily showed a strange disturbance of the water, rather like a large serpent swimming on the surface with wind whipping up spray around it. The film was examined by experts who could detect no trace of tampering, but the image was far from clear enough to convince sceptics that what Gray had photographed was more than a freak wave or a strangely twisted treetrunk.

Other pictures were just as inconclusive, but the following year the London *Daily Mail* published one that was to set the world alight, and which has appeared in most books about Nessie published since. This was the famous 'Surgeon's Picture' claimed to have been taken on 1 April 1934 by Dr R. Kenneth Wilson, a Harley Street gynaecologist, from a height of about 100ft (30m) above the loch and about three miles (5km) from Invermoriston on the road to Inverness. The picture showed the now familiar plesiosaur-type neck and small head rising out of the water.

To many this picture seemed to prove Nessie's existence beyond doubt, but almost exactly 60 years later the truth came out: an April Fool's jape had got out of control. By the time newspapers around the world had picked up on it, the hoaxers dared not confess the reality, which was that they had modelled a plastic-wood head and neck onto a 13in (32cm) toy submarine and carefully photographed it so no background would betray the scale. Wilson had not even taken the fake picture; he had agreed to act as front man because his professional status would impress.

This episode warns us against trusting too much in the respectability of witnesses, but only a terminal cynic could say that it proves the whole fuss at Loch Ness is based on lies.

One of the commonest places for Nessie sightings is off the shore by Urquhart Castle – aptly because it was probably St Columba's visit to the Pictish King Brude at Urquhart which gave us our earliest account of Nessie. There has been a stronghold on the site since the Iron Age; the ruins you can see there today are of a late-13th-century castle which became home to the Grant clan and was blown up in 1692 to prevent it falling into Jacobite hands.

OPPOSITE:

Nessie's brood

The loch is nearly 1,000ft (300m) deep at this point and there are rumours that there is an underwater cavern here where Nessie and her brood shelter. Suggestions that such caverns might lead to the ocean are implausible as the loch surface is some 50ft (15m) above sea-level.

Nahuelito

As Nessie is to Scotland, Nahuelito is to Argentina. Nahuelito is said to inhabit the large Nahuel Huapi Lake up in the Andes in the north of the province of Patagonia. Some say it looks like a serpent, others like a plesiosaur, and estimates of its length go up to over 100ft (30m). It is said to surface only in summer when the surface is calm, but occasionally it goes foraging on shore, leaving a trail of destruction; no clear casts have yet been taken of its footprints.

*Ancient carving
of Nahuelito*

Cynics may suspect plagiarism, but rumours of lake monsters go back as far among the Patagonian Indians as they do in Scotland – indeed, there was a major international hoo-ha about the Nahuel Huapi Monster in the 1920s, about 10 years before Loch Ness hit the headlines. Among several reports of a creature in Lake Nahuel Huapi was one by a respected US gold prospector, Martin Sheffield. He observed 'an animal with a huge neck like a swan, and the movements made me suppose the beast to have a body like that of a crocodile'. The then director of the Buenos Aires Zoo had for over 20 years received reports that there was some strange creature in the lake, and as a result of Sheffield's sighting launched an official expedition; alas, no concrete evidence was found. As at Loch Ness, the evidence has remained tantalizing, persistent but ultimately inconclusive.

OPPOSITE:

Patagonian lake monster

Ogopogo

North America has dozens of rumoured lake monsters. Among the better known are Igopogo (Lake Simcoe), Manipogo (Lake Manitoba), Ponik (Lake Pohénégamook) and the Turtle Lake Monster, but the most famous is Ogopogo, resident in Lake Okanagan in British Columbia, near the border with Washington State. There are Native American legends of a monster in the lake, and some early settler sightings date from 1872, but interest has really taken off only since the start of the

Ogopogo

20th century. There are now usually several sightings a year of a creature 30–50ft (9–15m) in length with a long thin neck, a rather horse-like head and an undulating, serpent-like body. Ogopogo can swim very fast, and often appears as several humps or even arches on the surface. Occasionally the creature looks like an upturned boat, which disconcerts descriptions of its serpent-like body, but no more so than with other lake monsters.

It is assumed that Ogopogo lives mainly on fish and weeds, but, in fact, the creature appears to be willing to eat almost anything, including horses and humans. Native Americans tell of the creature attacking humans, and some swimmers in the lake have disappeared without trace.

There are sightings from all parts of Lake Okanagan, which is 80 miles (130km) long, but most commonly these are from the area around Peachland. Native Americans believe Ogopogo – N'ha-a-itk, as they call the monster – inhabits a cave near Squally Point by Rattlesnake Island, which they used especially to avoid; in the old days, if they had to pass anywhere near this point they would take a live animal to throw overboard, and the early settlers continued this practice. They also patrolled the shores with guns to stop it coming ashore. The lake seems big enough for Ogopogo to continue to tease its admirers for some time to come – and under the protection of British Columbian law, which forbids anyone to harm the creature.

There are rumours of monsters in 38 other lakes in British Columbia, more than in any other Canadian province. Québec comes next, with about a dozen.

Champp

Lake Champlain in Vermont is another said to have a monster, generally described as about 30ft (9m) long and dark in colour. Its long neck is sometimes held out of the water, and its snake-like head has two short horns or ears.

Although dwarfed by the nearby Great Lakes, Lake Champlain is no pond, being about 100 miles (165km) long and up to 11 miles (18km) wide, with a depth of up to 400ft (120m). There are over 300 documented sightings of the creature, beginning with one in 1609 by Samuel de Champlain, who described Champ as a '20 foot [6m] serpent thick as a barrel and a head like a horse'. The local Iroquois described it as a 'horned serpent'. Mostly the creature seems quite harmless, although it is said to have chased a fishing boat to shore near Rouses Point in 1930. In 1983 the New York State Assembly passed a resolution forbidding harm to be done to the Lake Champlain Monster, so it has achieved official recognition of sorts.

The best time for sighting Champ is in the early morning in summer, when the weather is settled. On several occasions it has been seen by whole boatloads of passengers on pleasure steamers, as happened on 30 July 1984. The *Spirit of Ethan Allen* was passing Appletree Point with over 80 passengers aboard when Champ surfaced nearby. The creature showed three to five humps, each standing about a foot (30cm) from the surface. The skin was brown-green and slimy-looking. The length was estimated at about 30ft (9m). Champ swam alongside the steamer for about 1,000yd (900m) before an approaching speedboat scared it away.

Lake Seljord Monster

According to a contemporary statement by the ambassador of the Duke of Mosconia: 'the lake called Mos, and the Island of Hoffusen in the myddest thereof is in the degree 45.30 and 61. In this lake appeareth a strange monster, which is a serpent of huge bigness... It was seen of late in the year of Christ 1522, appearing far above the water, rowling like a great pillar, and was by conjecture far off esteemed to be of fifty cubits in length.'

The lakes of Scandinavia are as full of rumoured monsters as the seas. Known as the Seljordsorm, the monster – or *lindorm* – of Lake Seljord in the Telemark county of Norway is one of the most famous. The lake is one of the smallest to have a reputed monster, being barely nine miles (15km) long and little over a mile (2km) wide at its widest, with an average depth of about 180ft (60m), increasing to 500ft (160m) in

OPPOSITE:

Champ

Norwegian sea monster in cave

places. Many of the other lakes nearby might seem far more likely to harbour a monster, but the rumours at Lake Seljord have been persistent.

The earliest sighting of the Seljordsorm on record is from the summer of 1750, when the creature is said to have attacked one Gunleik Andersson-Verpe of Bø as he was rowing from Ulvneset to Garvikstrondi beach. He described the creature as a 'sea-horse'; it overturned his boat, but he managed to escape unharmed. For a while after this people

armed themselves before rowing out on the lake, but this appears to be the only violent incident on record. The monster still occasionally scares people, but it has not yet attacked them.

From the beginning the monster was often dismissed as an illusion, probably just a group of otters or beavers swimming in line; but in 1880 everyone was startled when Bjorn Bjorge and his mother claimed to have killed a baby specimen. They had been washing clothes in the lake when a strange lizard-like creature, 40in (1m) long, came swimming by. They killed it with a stick. The remains were left to rot on the beach for the curiosity of locals, but sadly no one thought to preserve any bones which might identify it.

Sightings continued, most witnesses describing the creature as dark with a light underside, resembling 'a serpent with a horse-like head', which it often raises 40in (1m) or so above the surface. Some people have described the head as like that of a lizard or crocodile; one such witness, Eivind Fjodstuft, saw it ashore. In 1920 he was out fishing one calm day when he saw a large creature lumbering out of the lake onto the shore. When it noticed him it slid back into the water and swam towards him. Fjodstuft later sketched what he saw and described the creature as 50–60ft (15–20m) long, with a head rather like a crocodile's. It had fin-like forefeet and was black, with no visible facial features. Others have also seen 'fins' when the creature spins on the surface.

Some have said the monster is even longer, but most witnesses say the Lake Seljord Monster is smaller than 15m (50ft), and shows three or four 'humps' when on the surface. Interest boomed in the 1930s and sightings have increased in number, partly through determined observation and partly because the lake has become more popular and accessible. Some film has been taken of the monster, but nothing that is clear enough to stand as proof.

In 1977 Operation Selma, or Expedition 77, was launched by Jan-Ove Sundberg, Adolf Refvik and Oystein Molstad-Andresen to gather evidence about the monster. Among the dozens of plausible witness accounts they harvested is that of Ivar Hesmyr. On Easter Monday 1977 he was fishing in a small boat with his 13-year-old daughter, Solveig and a neighbour's son when suddenly three gleaming humps rose out of the water only a hundred or so yards (91m) away; Hesmyr estimated them as adding up to about 30ft (10m) in all. Beyond the humps rose a small head on a long neck. The only details of the head they could make out before the creature began swimming away from them were small, cat-like ears. Apparently the creature swam very fast, fast enough to raise a bow-wave. Hesmyr's daughter screamed, and when he looked up from comforting her the monster had disappeared. His daughter said the humps had sunk first, then the neck and head. When they reached shore, Hesmyr swore never to go out on the lake again. He noted that he had never doubted the monster's existence, but neither had he ever expected to come so close.

The same monster was seen by other witnesses that year. In fact, 1977 was a bumper year for sightings, but what the survey showed most interestingly was that the monster had been regularly spotted for years, and this pattern has continued since, with a high level of credibility in the witnesses.

The creature is most often seen in the bay near Seljord village (population about 3,000). This is partly, one supposes, because the population is densest there, but also it may be because of a fish-rich estuary there which connects with Lake Sundsbarm to the north. Like Loch Ness, the lake is rich in salmon trout and eels, and it is guessed that the monster feeds largely on these. In July 1986 Bjarne Haugstol spotted a three-humped monster chasing a shoal of fish near Lauvsnes and described the water in front of the humps as 'boiling' with them.

Folklore says the creature originally lived in a small lake called Östertjonn in the mountains overlooking Seljord. When it outgrew this modest abode, it slithered down Rausberget mountain into the main lake, leaving a track still visible many years later.

Lake Storsjön Monster

On the dark bottom of the great salt lake
Imprisoned lies the giant snake,
With naught his sullen sleep to break
Norse poem translated by Henry Wadsworth Longfellow

Lake Storsjön is the fifth largest lake in Sweden, lying in a fairly remote area some 300 miles (500km) north and slightly west of Stockholm. It is said to contain a creature which in Sweden is often called simply the Great Lake Monster. Since 1987 the Society for Investigating the Great Lake has collected some 400 reports of 'Storsjödjuret', as the Swedes also call it, dating from 1635 to the present. Most sightings date from the end of the 19th century, when it was seen several times on land, and from the last few decades. At one time people were warned against planting vegetables too close to the lake because they might attract the monster.

The overall impression given by witnesses is of a creature 10–25ft (3–8m) long and 3–5ft (1–1.5m) wide. Sometimes it resembles an upturned boat, sometimes a log; sometimes it takes the classic lake-monster profile with three humps, a long neck and a small head. The head has been variously compared to that of a horse, dog, lizard and snake. The creature has stubby legs or fins on which it can go ashore. It appears to swim very fast, up to 15 knots (28kph), and sometimes it makes a curious sound like two pieces of wood clapping against each other. Storsjödjuret is seen most often on sunny evenings in July, August and September.

Besides the usual theories, a popular local proposition is that it may be a giant catfish, because some reports mention whiskers that might be barbels. Experts believe this unlikely, not just on the grounds of size but because catfish generally need warm water in which to reproduce, and Lake Storsjön is cold. However, a degree of local adaptation is not impossible and the record length for a catfish in Sweden is over 10ft (3m).

A firm convert to the catfish theory was Ragnar Bjork. In August 1973, aged 68, he heard a commotion down on the lake. He suspected poachers and, being a lake warden, went to investigate. He steered his boat towards Sikskaret and, when the engine cut out, took to the oars. After a while he saw something sticking out of the water and waving oddly. It turned out to be the dorsal fin and back of a fish 20ft (6m) long, half as long again as his own boat. In terror he stood up and hit it across the back with an oar. The fish lashed back with its tail and the boat 'flew through the air', luckily landing the right way up. When Ragnar summoned the courage to look the fish had vanished. He swore it was a giant catfish, and described the head as long, narrow and flat. The 'barbels' were, he said, 5ft (1.5m) long. The creature had gills and was black on top, yellow underneath.

If it can leave the water, though, the Great Lake Monster is unlikely to be a catfish. Perhaps there are both giant catfish and other monsters in Storsjön. Interviewed in 1994, Karl-Olov Johansson described a monster he had seen in Brunflovikan Bay in 1910. Walking by the lake one June afternoon he noticed that a strange creature in a meadow on the opposite shore of the bay was making its way down to the water:

'It didn't move as any known animal. It crawled and at the same time its back went up and down.'

He estimated the length as 13–16ft (4–5m). It stood about 40in (1m) high and its body was short and thick, narrowing at both ends. The creature, which was dark grey, appeared to have no neck, the head being right on the body, and there was something moving under the body which might have been feet, but the distance was too great for him to be sure. The monster swam out into the lake, gradually sinking and disappearing.

Every year brings fresh sightings. In June 1997 Stefan Wickstrom went night-fishing in Brunflo Bay with two friends in a cabin cruiser. Shortly after midnight, the back of some enormous creature surfaced about 55yd (50m) off to one side of them. They estimated it to be 30–60ft (10–20m) long and thought it was greyish-black and featureless. Reassuring his friends that the Great Lake Monster had never attacked anyone, Wickstrom steered towards it but before he reach it had sunk and disappeared.

LAKE MONSTERS

OPPOSITE:

Frösön Island in Lake Storsjön has been inhabited since prehistoric times when it was consecrated to Frö, the local goddess of love and fertility.

Among the many ancient monuments on the island stands an enigmatic runestone which is said to bind the monster in the lake until such time as someone deciphers its inscription.

5

EPILOGUE

Tyrannosaurus Rex

Monsters are always good for a thrill — especially fictional ones, where the threat is purely imaginary. Jules Verne, H.G. Wells and Sir Arthur Conan Doyle livened up literature with some notable monsters around the turn of the 19th century, but the invention of cinema added a fresh crop of characters to popular culture: King Kong, Godzilla, the Creature from the Black Lagoon ... Fictional monsters don't have to be all that credible to be fun. The more fanciful the creature's genesis, the more outrageous can be its adventures:

It had seemed such a good idea at the time, during the nuclear-hostile backlash that followed Chernobyl. There was this rocky node in the Celtic fringe of the UK that happened to be naturally radioactive. Well, a small mountain really. Curiously, the same mountain that Arthurian myth spoke of as having two dragons curled at the root, a red dragon and a white one, whose struggles kept destroying a castle some king or other had tried to build on it. It's strange how true some old myths turn out to be. Not that many people on the project had ever heard the legend, and none of them thought it more than a faintly amusing coincidence.

Anyway, back to the point, which was that there was this mountain in Wales which was highly radioactive at its cave-riddled root. Naturally radioactive. What's more, the Ministry of Defence already happened to own a large slice of it. Where better to build a subterranean complex in which unpopular research could be carried out well away from prying eyes? At the same time, equipment and clothing and humans themselves could be tested working in a highly radioactive environment, ready for the next Chernobyl. Not only that but, when the work was done, what a handy place to dispose of some of the increasingly embarrassing piles of waste from power stations. The logic seemed unassailable. Some pro-nuclear evangelists in the Ministry were even tempted to go public with the scheme and win the nation's support, but they were overruled.

It's easy to be wise after the event. One cannot blame the instigators too much. Possibly a decade or two earlier they would have had public approval for the project. The argument was a powerful one: since the place had always been so radioactive anyway, what harm would adding a tiny bit more do?

The big flaw was something which no one could possibly have guessed. They couldn't know that the radiation that had brought them tunnelling steeply down through the hillside had also for countless ages been patiently carrying out its own agenda; blindly (unless one takes the view that all events in the universe are directed by hidden powers) performing the most subtle alchemy on the creature which fate had dropped into its maw; tinkering with the structure of its cells and molecules and even the atoms making up those molecules, keeping a spark of strange dormant life alight in them.

Deep-sea volcano

And all the while the creature itself had been dreaming strange dreams, its spirit tethered like a balloon to a carcass that should by now have crystallized to stone, but had instead metamorphosed into a new form of life, totally sidestepping evolution to produce a monster beyond the normal bounds of nature.

Even then things might have gone as planned were it not for the explosion that cracked open the beast's sarcophagus and shook it out of its strange saurian dreams. It might have continued to dream for the next ten million years if it had not been woken. But there was the explosion. Suddenly the beast had been shaken out of its dreams. Ravenous with hunger, eager for life and the light which had been denied it, it clawed its way up from the depths and burst upon a startled world …

Nigelosaur Bobaltonatrops
at 20,000 leagues.

The above is a sketch for an illustrated short story with which we had rather hoped to conclude this book. In the event, time, space and several other considerations prevented this; but the pictures are too good to waste so we are showing them as a taster of what Bob can do in this line. Anyone who would like to see more is advised to seek out the series of *Godzilla* digest novels he has illustrated, published by Random House and aimed at young adults.

This is a line of work he loves, as it is closely related to the monster movies for which he has a passion. He has over 1,000 titles in his own video collection and has provided most of the information for the following quick review.

Among his favourite films is the classic *Beast from 20,000 Fathoms* (1953), directed by Eugene Lourie and with·impressive special effects by Ray Harryhausen, the acknowledged master of the art for several decades. The story, based on *The Fog Horn* by Ray Bradbury, tells of a 'rhedosaurus' (a totally fictional breed of dinosaur) being

unfrozen by atom-bomb testing in the Arctic, and then going on to wreck New York. Eugene Lourie directed two further classics about giant dinosaurs emerging from the sea, *The Giant Behemoth* (1959) and *Gorgo* (1961). These were UK productions, which meant it was London's turn to be gleefully reduced to rubble. The first two movies used stop-frame animation for the monster, which many consider more realistic than the 'man in a rubber suit' employed for *Gorgo*, but that movie has its own charm. In it the monster is brought back to life by an erupting volcano. The trouble starts when her baby is captured and put on show as a sea monster in a London circus. The mother, ten times larger, naturally goes looking for it …

Essentially the same plot was used some years later in the Japanese film *Gappa – The Trifibian Monster* (1967), released in the United States as *Monster from a Prehistoric Planet*. Gappa is only one of many Japanese movie monsters that rise out of the sea. The most famous (or infamous) is of course the home-grown Godzilla (Gojira), Japan's answer to King Kong. Godzilla is a vast sea monster, part dinosaur, part other things, that first appeared in the Toho film *Gojira* (1954), which means literally 'Gorilla Whale', and proved so popular that over the next 20 years there followed a dense series of films made by Toho Studios. Then came a lull until 1984, when a new set of seven movies was made, ending when the poor monster was killed off in *Godzilla vs. Destroyer* (1995). However, like Dracula, Godzilla was not to be so easily disposed of. TriStar Pictures resurrected our friend in the $90 million movie *Godzilla* (1998), giving him a complete makeover and using the latest Computer Graphics Imaging for a realism that Harryhausen could only have dreamt of.

Speaking as someone with a more than passing knowledge of the subject, Eggleton says of Godzilla's appeal:

'Godzilla is simply a force of nature. Lately we have been seeing people mess around with nature. They screw around with DNA, virus mutations and radiation, and while I'm not against this, too many people are doing it without a clue as to the outcome. As Dr Yamane states in the original version of *Godzilla*, Godzilla was "a product of the H-bomb", and his footsteps bear traces of strontium-90. Godzilla is nature's reaction to mankind's recklessness. He is a reluctant hero trapped in a world he never made. In fact, we made him and now we see him as a nuisance. That's why some of the 1960s Godzilla films were great, like *Godzilla vs. The Sea Monster* (1966), where he just sort of lived on a remote island and bothered no one until they bothered him. And he ultimately saves humanity without them really giving him credit. He is also an antihero. He is simple, primal fury in a complex nothing-is-as-it-seems world. We'd all like to be like him: simpler. Not to mention knocking a few buildings down when we get pissed off.'

Eggleton's personal favourite of the first series of films is *Invasion of the Astro Monster* (1965), which has been released also as *Battle of the Astros*, *Godzilla vs. Monster Zero*, *Invasion of Planet X*, and *Monster Zero* – indeed, almost all the Godzilla movies have had a bewildering array of variant titles.

In 1966, the rival Daiei Studios produced *Daikaiju Gamera* with their own monster, Gamera, who was (wait for it) a giant fire-breathing turtle who could swim underwater or fly through the air like a rocket, and was especially protective towards children. Gamera never quite matched Godzilla's popularity, but it starred in a string of moderately successful films until 1971 when the studio went out of business. In 1995, Gamera was rescued from oblivion in *Gamera: Guardian of the Universe*; here the giant turtle is created in lost Atlantis, floats around unconscious as an 'island' until activated by

OPPOSITE:

Loose in the city

a runestone on its back, then wakes to save the world from the evil monster Gyaos. It is interesting to note that in this incarnation the story borrows from several old myths and legends we have considered earlier in this book.

The most famous US water monster is probably the one in *The Creature from the Black Lagoon* (1954), *Revenge of the Creature* (1954) and *The Creature Walks Among Us* (1956). These movies departed from the usual formula by making the creature humanoid and of roughly human size: many larger monsters that in theory should have been more scary have somehow failed to move audiences the same way. Consider *The She Creature* (1956), *Monster from the Ocean Floor* (1954), *Creature from the Haunted Sea* (1956) and *Destination Inner Space* (1966).

US moviemakers have generally had more luck with 'real' sea monsters, such as the giant squid which stole the show in Disney's *20,000 Leagues Under the Sea* (1954), directed by Richard Fleischer and starring James Mason and Kirk Douglas, and the great white shark in Spielberg's *Jaws* (1975), which still causes nightmares twenty-odd years later.

UK moviemakers scored with *Warlords of Atlantis* (1978), in which some Victorian adventurers find that the Atlanteans (who originally lived on a moon of Mars that crashed into Earth) have survived in an underwater city. Among other marvels and monsters that the heroes encounter is a giant octopus which pursues them to the surface and proceeds to demolish their ship. Another 1970s UK venture that might have livened up the film monster scene but sadly failed to make it into production was *Nessie*, an intended collaboration between the famous Hammer Studios and Toho, the parent studio of Godzilla. The storyline involved Nessie being accidentally exposed to a growth hormone, escaping into the ocean from her loch and going on to threaten the whole world. More recently there has been the feature *Loch Ness* (1995), for which the monster was made by Jim Henson's Creature Workshop.

Such movies may seem a long way from the Midgard Serpent and Leviathan. It is true they are much more playful than the ancient myths, which were shaped over generations and for a long time were actually believed by those who heard them; but the underlying appeal is not so different. The message or metaphor is much the same. Monsters from the deep still mean to us what they did to our ancestors, even when they are being used merely for dramatic effect in entertainment.

Fantasy has always enriched itself by feeding on fact and serious legend. In a way, Bob Eggleton has proved with his illustrations for this book that the reverse can also happen. He came to the subject through an ongoing love, begun in childhood, for dinosaurs, monster movies and fantasy monsters generally. Now he has used that love and his talent to breathe fresh life into the foundation on which Godzilla and the like rest.

The chances are that, if you have read this far, you will need no persuading about how well Eggleton's 'Turneresque' style suits the subject of sea monsters. Just as Turner and the later Impressionists shattered the realist veneer of Victorian painting to show a new and often more powerful way of portraying things, Eggleton in the field of modern fantasy art demonstrates how the energy of a subject can often be released more effectively by not rendering it in the photographic detail which is now taken for granted. As with all techniques, much depends on the skill and intent of the user; and it is even likely that sometime in the future he will return to photorealism. But in his illustrations for this book there is an implicit challenge from Eggleton to his fellow illustrators: try throwing away your airbrushes and computers and just do it with paint and brush!

OPPOSITE:

Giant jellyfish

As for myself, I too had a prior interest in the topic. I have spent time watching the sun rise over Loch Ness. I have a plausible enough photograph of a large smooth object breaking the surface of Loch Morar one misty morning (sadly just a rock, as the dispersing mist soon revealed – unless the creature was extraordinarily patient and waited until we left before making a move).

For a while as a child in Africa, I was convinced I had discovered an unknown monster in the Zambezi River, near which we lived. With hindsight, I reckon it must have been a crocodile with unusual markings – and that was the opinion of the river warden I fruitlessly tried to persuade to come and see it – but at the time I wasn't convinced, because I knew very well what crocodiles looked like and I had seen this creature at close quarters on two separate occasions, peering down at it from a fallen tree just above the water. So, in a modest way, I sympathize with the sea captain who, when his crew reported a sea serpent nearby, refused to leave his cabin: if the serpent was real, he said, he didn't want to be laughed at for the rest of his life for admitting having seen it.

So it was a great pleasure to be able to plunge into the subject in some detail in this book, and even more fun to see it take shape as Eggleton's wonderful pictures rolled in. The only drawback is that, because of writing this book I find myself more wary than ever of setting foot in the sea; if it ever falls into my daughter's hands it will put her off for life. We had a hard enough time last summer explaining away all the yard-wide jellyfish on the beach …

Artist's Acknowledgements

First, a thank you, dear reader, for picking up this book. Were it not for the following other people, this book would never have been:

Thanks to J.M.W. Turner, Thomas Moran, Albert Bierstadt and Winslow Homer for what you left for me to be inspired by – if only you knew now what the world knows (and I know) about you four, and what your long-forgotten critics never did know.

Thanks to Mark Collins and Cameron Brown for going ahead with what for several years, and with several publishers, was an off-again-on-again project. My heartfelt thanks to Cindy Richards, Muna Reyal, Sonia Pugh, Terry Shaughnessy and Paul Barnett for taking this book in the right direction. Thanks to John Strange and Megra Mitchell for their always unexpected but wonderful and flowing design work, Thanks (again) to Nigel Suckling, whose historical knowledge made this book be something other than a bunch of pictures.

My thanks, and heart, to Marianne for the encouragement, research and ideas that helped add the finishing touches ....

And to all the people who said, 'Yeah, but you can only paint spacescapes, Bob' ... thanks. So there.

Bob Eggleton and the publishers would also like to thank the The Map Room, The Royal Library, Copenhagen for the use of Abraham Ortelius' *Teatrum Orbis Terrarum* on page 8.

About the Artist

Bob Eggleton was born on 13 September 1960. At an early age he was fascinated by science fiction and fantasy of all types, and in particular by monster movies featuring Godzilla and other creatures. He attended Rhode Island College and left to pursue a career in commercial illustration and fine art.

He is now one of the most sought-after fantasy artists in the business, having been published in the United States, Europe and Japan. A keen traveller, he has recently ventured around the planet and has walked and flown over active volcanoes in Hawaii and climbed sheer cliff faces in Australia.

Originally known as an artist of space subjects, he then came back to planet Earth for more fantasy-oriented imagery, although willing to return to space at any time. He has written and drawn comic books and illustrated children's books, and was a conceptual artist on the Las Vegas thrill ride Star Trek: The Experience. He contributed conceptualizations to the movie *Sphere* (1998), based on the 1987 Michael Crichton book.

Eggleton has illustrated for nearly every publisher of science fiction, fantasy and horror. His work has earned him seven Chesley Awards (given by the Association of SF/Fantasy Artists) and three Hugo Awards. He is a frequent Guest of Honour at science fiction conventions, a role he will fulfil again at the World Science Fiction Convention in 2000AD.

His *Alien Horizons: The Fantastic Art of Bob Eggleton* (1995) with Nigel Suckling was a Science Fiction Book Club bestseller. Bob has also illustrated a hugely successful series of Godzilla™ books, published by Random House.

About the Author

Nigel Suckling was born in 1950 in Africa, in what was then called Northern Rhodesia and is now Zambia. He moved to Britain at the age of sixteen and went on to study Engineering at Imperial College, London. Since then, he has spent most of his time and energy on various aspects of fantasy art.

He first began to write for the Paper Tiger list in 1983 when Rodney Matthews asked him to compose the text for *In Search of Forever* and has since written many profiles of fantasy artists including Bob Eggleton, Wayne Anderson, Linda and Roger Garland, Josh Kirby and Jürgen Ziewe. Nigel has also written *Heroic Dreams* and *The Book of the Unicorn* among many others and is currently planning an illustrated book on vampires.

Other occupations when necessity has called include commercial and educational illustration, editing and a colourful variety of other jobs of the type that actors turn to when 'resting'.

Selected Further Reading

Bousfield, Edward, and LeBlond, Paul: *Cadborosaurus: Survivor from the Deep*, Horsdal & Schubert, 1994

Bright, Michael: *There Are Giants in the Sea*, Robson, 1989

Costello, Peter: *In Search of Lake Monsters*, Granada, 1975

Dinsdale, Tim: *The Leviathans*, Routledge & Kegan Paul, 1966

Dinsdale, Tim: *Loch Ness Monster*, Routledge & Kegan Paul, 1966; revised 1976

Ellis, Richard: *Monsters of the Sea*, Doubleday, 1995

Gould, Charles: *Mythical Monsters*, W.H. Allen, 1886

Gould, Rupert T.: *The Case for the Sea Serpent*, Philip Allan, 1930

Heuvelmans, Bernard: *In the Wake of the Sea Serpents*, Rupert Hart-Davis, 1968

Ley, Willy: *The Lungfish, the Dodo and the Unicorn*, Viking, 1949

Lum, Peter: *Fabulous Beasts*, Pantheon Books, 1951

McEwan, Graham J.: *Sea Serpents, Sailors and Sceptics*, Routledge & Kegan Paul, 1978

Meurger, Michel, and Gagnon, Claude: *Lake Monster Traditions: A Cross-Cultural Analysis*, Fortean Tomes, 1988 (much expanded and revised from Monstres des lacs du Québec: mythes et troublantes réalités, Stanké, Montréal, 1982)

Spence, Lewis: *History of Atlantis*, Rider, 1926